Healing
the
Wounds
of
Divorce

Other Books by Barbara Leahy Shlemon
Published by Ave Maria Press:

◆ HEALING PRAYER
◆ HEALING THE HIDDEN SELF
◆ TO HEAL AS JESUS HEALED
(with Dennis and Matthew Linn)

Healing *the* Wounds *of* Divorce

—— A ——

SPIRITUAL GUIDE TO RECOVERY

BARBARA LEAHY SHLEMON

AVE MARIA PRESS   Notre Dame, Indiana 46556

© 1992 by Ave Maria Press, Notre Dame, IN 46556

International Standard Book Number: 0-87793-483-5

Library of Congress Catalog Card Number: 92-71294

Cover and text design by Katherine Robinson Coleman

Printed and bound in the United States of America.

"The dead man came out, his feet and hands bound with bands of stuff and a cloth round his face. Jesus said to them, 'Unbind him, let him go free'" (Jn 11:44).

*This book is affectionately dedicated
to my adult sons and daughters,
Christopher, Steven, Beth, Amy, and David.*

My heart will be eternally grateful for the unconditional love shown to your divorced parents by remaining true to your promise to "not take sides."

CONTENTS

PROLOGUE 9

ONE
Denial 17

TWO
Rejection 23

THREE
Fear 29

FOUR
Grief 35

FIVE
Anger 43

SIX
Shame 51

SEVEN
Guilt 59

EIGHT
Children 65

NINE
Finances 73

TEN
Relatives 77

ELEVEN
Loneliness 83

TWELVE
Friendship 89

THIRTEEN
Intimacy 95

FOURTEEN
Dating 99

FIFTEEN
Self-Esteem 105

SIXTEEN
Forgiveness 111

SEVENTEEN
Surrender 117

EPILOGUE 123

APPENDIX
Annulment 125

NOTES 133

FURTHER READING 134

PROLOGUE

My heart was pounding wildly inside my chest as I climbed the stairs and entered the sparsely furnished one bedroom apartment that was to be my home for the next four months. It smelled of stale cigarette smoke, the windows were in need of cleaning and the carpet was very worn in spots. The small space felt uncomfortable and uninviting.

How did I get to this place? After thirty years of marriage, five children, and a twenty-year career of Christian ministry why was I living alone in an ugly apartment building? The feelings of despair, anxiety, and disorientation were enormous as I sat on the worn out sofa and tried to reconstruct the events of the past several months.

Ben and I separated in November and it was he who initially found this apartment and moved into it while I remained on the other side of town in the family home. The separation came after many years of distress in trying to make the marriage work. We attended Marriage Encounter, went on couples' retreats, sought help through counseling, and talked endlessly about the situation, always trying to discover some way to breach the wall between us.

We always agreed on one thing: we were capable of rearing beautiful children. Our energy, attention, and love were focused in that direction. From that standpoint our union was not a failure. But the years of living together did not promote a deepening in our love for each other. We grew farther and farther apart in our activities, our social life, and our spiritual life.

In the end we simply decided to stop making one another so unhappy. There was no rancor, we didn't hate each other, but finally we could no longer continue to live our lives in isolation from one another while pretending to play the role of a happily married couple. In many ways it would have been simpler if there were wild arguments and terrible confrontations, then our children, other family members, and friends would have expected the break-up of the marriage. But we avoided such scenes, preferring to exist under the same roof in a kind of silent rage, dwelling in the same house, yet living separate existences.

When it became too painful, too intense, and too depressing to live with such dishonesty, we made the decision to separate. For several months I stayed in the family home. But my travel schedule took me out of town nearly every week, making it necessary for Ben to pick up the mail, watch the house, and cut the lawn. It seemed only logical to trade living arrangements.

While I was living in our home, there were visits from family and friends. I had plenty of room for someone to come for a meal or stay overnight. Now I would be living alone, really alone, for the first time in my entire life. I had always considered myself a fairly confident person who met the challenges of life with optimism and a strong faith in God's constant abiding presence, but this situation was proving otherwise. As I sat on the sofa my emotions were on overload and my response was to shut down all my feelings a condition I describe as "numbing out." My mind was dissociating from all feelings. A kind of catatonic shock took over, creating an interior vacuum of nothing-ness, like being swallowed up in a black hole.

I don't recall how long I sat there, but the sun was going down when I finally became conscious of the lengthening shadows on the brick wall opposite the living room window. I realized the day was nearly over and I had not eaten anything. The truth of the matter was, I had given up eating because I equated mealtime with sharing conversation and I hated eating alone. Nevertheless, I forced myself to walk across the street to the large supermarket and buy something to put in the refrigerator. This experience created even greater havoc in my heart.

Walking up and down the aisles crammed with food, I was at a loss to know what to buy. I had never bought groceries only for myself. I honestly did not know what I liked to eat. "This is crazy," I thought to myself. "Of course I know what I like." But the truth was I did not. As I stood in the last aisle, staring at the loaves of bread, the sub-merged feelings of isolation, rejection, and aloneness came rising to the surface and I began to sob. "Lord," I cried, "I don't know who I am or what I like or why I'm here. I'm so frightened. Please help!"

I left the store without buying anything and went back to the apartment where I cried so long and so loud I was afraid the neighbors would call the police. The pain of that day broke down my resistance to feelings and I began to encounter emotions I had previously denied.

I didn't think the human body was capable of discharg-ing so many tears. For hours at a time my heartbeat was noticeably erratic, accompanied by strong pains in my chest. I would wake up in the middle of the night with panic attacks, an inability to breathe, and irrational fears. I would walk through the apartment checking the locks on the doors and windows, often falling asleep again with the TV and lights on to keep me company.

Dreams of being chased and killed were nightly occurrences. I seldom awoke feeling rested. The muscles in my neck and shoulders were so tense that no amount of exercise or massage would bring relief. I prayed to die rather than spend the remainder of my life in so much mental, spiritual, and physical trauma. It felt like total devastation and desolation.

Three years later I can still vividly recall that period of my life. Time has not dimmed the memories of despair that tormented many of my days and nights. However, I am no longer paralyzed by these powerful emotions. God has slowly been restoring me to a wholeness I didn't know existed. The process of recovery from the pain of divorce has broadened my understanding of God, myself, and others. Although I didn't realize it at the time, I now see divorce as the instrument which God used to allow me to become more honest about myself and, therefore, more honest in my relationships.

Learning to know "who I am" has proved to be the greatest challenge because I had become comfortable in being what others needed me to be. These traits were established early in my life as a means of protecting against the pain of growing up in a non-nurturing family. I learned to adapt in order to be liked, regardless of how adapting made me feel. This dishonesty also made it difficult to initiate and maintain healthy relationships. How could I successfully bond with another if I was afraid to be my real self? My inner search revealed the fact that I truly did not know what a healthy union between two persons looked like. My competence to choose a mate for life was blocked by my incompetence in knowing myself. I now believe my motives for entering into marriage were severely defective. I wasn't looking for a mate as much as searching for a father.

The divorce forced me to take a good look at Barbara. Instead of the accomplished woman I presented to the world, I had to uncover the frightened child within who never felt loved and accepted for herself. I had to stop believing that a failed marriage meant my entire life was a failure. I have now come to realize that recovering from the trauma of divorce is not only a possibility, but a reality. There is life after death, even while we are still on this earth.

The divorce experience also gave me new insights about prayer and increased my understanding of the Good Shepherd's willingness to "look for the lost one, bring back the stray, bandage the wounded and make the weak strong" (Ez 34:16). Even in the darkest moments of despair, I knew God was not abandoning me.

I'm nowhere near completing this task, but at least I'm on the journey . . . the journey of a lifetime. Depending on the choices made, divorce can be a passage to deeper truths, or it can be a road that leads nowhere. Some choose to rebuild their lives on more solid ground, using wisdom born of sorrow to guide the construction. Others decide to avoid even the semblance of closeness to another. Most people who make it through see themselves as real survivors.

"Divorce has the potential not only of freeing men and women from destructive and unsatisfactory relationships, but of allowing adults to develop and change in gratifying ways in the aftermath of divorce," states Joan Kelly of the California Children of Divorce Project. "The majority of men and women followed beyond the separation period reported that the divorce was a positive and necessary step which resulted in greater personal contentment, increased self esteem, and healthier levels of psychological functioning."

My own experience taught me that divorce recovery was largely up to me. Was I willing to do the inner work of looking honestly at myself? Did I want to open up all those feelings again? Did I really desire to have God heal me of the pain?

It took me a long time to come to grips with my feelings, to understand how my emotions related to my spiritual life. I was accustomed to finding God in the silence and peace of a tranquil spirit, so how was I to relate to the Lord in the midst of this chaos?

Had I been abandoned by the Creator too? Was the choice to separate and divorce an unforgivable and unpardonable sin that doomed me to hell? The good news is that the reality of the moral implications of separation and divorce have been addressed by theologians. Those who are struggling with such questions may want to read some of the current literature on the subject. (Several excellent books are suggested in the "Further Reading" section.) I also found great comfort in discussing my fears with priests and ministers who are familiar with modern interpretations of scripture relating to divorce.

I am not qualified to write about the canonical rules and laws governing the status of divorced persons. However, in the past three years I have learned a few things about the psycho/spiritual/social problems presented by divorce. I have come to recognize the need to stay connected to God in order to maintain spiritual awareness and continued nurturing.

To feel cut off, disowned, or condemned by the one who created us adds a heavy burden of sorrow to a heart already weighed down with sadness. Sometimes this sense of alienation from the God of love is the final straw that brings about emotional breakdown, depression, or suicide. During my personal search for support and direction, I found little literature outside of the Bible to comfort and console my broken spirit. There is much material describing the psychological and sociological experience of divorce, but not a great deal written to assist the process of spiritual healing.

However, most divorced people I queried in researching this book feel their deepest sense of isolation is in regard to their relationship to God and to the church. This overwhelming sense of no longer feeling connected to God seems to be true for Protestants and Catholics alike. This feeling of abandonment can promote the inner conviction of divorce as a tragedy evoking only defeat and darkness, making it impossible to move on with life.

I also found most of the literature available on the subject of divorce much too sophisticated and complex for one whose mind is on emotional overload. Reading lengthy explanations of divorce recovery was impossible for me in the months following our separation. My concentration was minimal and my ability to retain information nearly non-existent.

Therefore, this book is written in a meditation style, with a short explanation and accompanying prayer for each area of difficulty. I hope that the reader will derive comfort and consolation through this process. I write this from my own woundedness, sharing from my heart and believing the peace of Jesus will continue to heal the author as well as the reader.

CHAPTER ONE

Denial

Denial is like two fish swimming in the ocean. They probed the coral reefs, examined aquatic vegetation, swam for many miles. Finally one fish asked, "What are we looking for?" The other answered, "I heard there is water down here someplace."

A person in denial is incapable of perceiving reality. Others can see it very readily and may even point out the danger signs. "Mary, you are in a destructive relationship." But Mary has become adept at denying her feelings regarding the abusive treatment. "He's just going through a rough time right now. I have to be patient with him." Often it takes some form of strong intervention by a professional counselor, trusted friend, or compassionate minister before a person is jolted into seeing the truth in an honest way.

Denial is a common way of dealing with painful situations. The Irish have practiced a type of survival mechanism for centuries by using the phrase, "It could have been worse." No matter what the situation, regardless of the suffering, despite any sign of hope, this phrase in invoked to cover any and all subjects. The loss of a job, the death of a loved one, a diagnosis of cancer always elicit the same attitude. A clear message is given, "You have no right to be upset over this event because others are suffering far more than you." "This is not as terrible as you think it is." "Ignore the problem, accept it as your cross in life, stop feeling sorry for yourself." The Irish have no corner on this kind of thinking, but we have made a science out of it.

Great damage is done when a person continues to bury her head in sand in this manner. Reality is distorted. One plays the game of trying to live honestly with dishonesty.

Coming out of denial can be extremely difficult because a person is very often in denial about the denial. I remember the first time I went through a seminar about dysfunctional families. I spent a lot of time sympathizing with all the participants at the workshop who admitted living in unhealthy relationships. At no time during the entire day did I personally identify with any of the information being taught or the pain being shared in the group.

One year later, after experiencing a period of emotional burnout that finally wore down my defenses, I faced the reality of my less than perfect marriage. When the pain became more intense than my fears, I opened my eyes to the truth. Once again I made the same workshop, given by the same therapist, using the same material, and I was amazed at the way it described my family. The teachings were pertinent to every detail of my life.

My initial exposure to this reality had not penetrated my defense system until I first experienced an emotional upheaval that woke me up and got my attention. I could finally see the water I had been swimming in all along. It was a frightening revelation. I was like Rip Van Winkle waking up after a long sleep and discovering the world had changed.

This awakening taught me about the deceitfulness of denial. The human mind can learn how to distort incoming data until it comes out looking entirely different. The classic illustration of this mechanism is known as the "hippopotamus in the living room" syndrome. In this scenario the hippo has obviously established residency in the home but no one is willing to admit its existence. Instead the family members walk around it, decorate it, put slip covers over it, build on another room to accommodate it, but never, ever do they say to one another, "There's a hippo in the living room." Such a silly metaphor may seem ridiculous, yet that is exactly the way a person in denial behaves. The unhealthy marital situation may be obvious to even casual acquaintances, but the marriage partners continue to pretend all is well.

Getting it straight and being honest takes courage because the consequences are enormous. There can be no more lying to yourself or others and you can no longer tolerate the destructive behavior. It means change and most of us dislike and avoid change. It's been said with much wisdom in the humor that the only person who really likes change is a wet baby.

Coming out of denial is frightening because we have no clear understanding of where the path will lead. There are no guarantees that peace will come through acceptance of the truth. In fact, the truth normally causes emotional chaos in the initial stages because we feel bombarded by insights previously filtered out of the mind.

But relief cannot be given until there is willingness to walk through the mayhem because awareness is the beginning of healing. The Christian faith teaches us to trust in Jesus Christ and his promise to never leave us or forsake us. During my journey out of denial I often played a song that reminded me of the constant presence of the Lord during my darkest moments of despair. These words were repeated continuously, "I'll never, no never, no never let go of your hand." At first I thought these were my words to the Lord but I soon realized they were his words to me. Jesus promised to remain with me forever and never abandon me, no matter what the situation may be.

The Lord fully understands the human trait of denial. When the disciples questioned Jesus about his use of parables in teaching the people, he replied with a marvelous illustration of the mechanism of denial. "I talk to them in parables because they look without seeing and listen without hearing or understanding. So in their case this prophesy of Isaiah is being fulfilled:

> "You will listen and listen again, but not understand,
> see and see again, but not perceive.
> For the heart of this nation has grown coarse,
> their ears are dull of hearing, and they have shut their eyes,
> for fear they should see with their eyes,
> hear with their ears,
> understand with their heart,
> and be converted
> and be healed by me"(Mt 13:13-15).

Facing the truth in an unhealthy marriage means confronting yourself and your spouse. The infrastructure is broken down and renovation must take place. One of the Twelve Step axioms as modified by the group Codependents Anonymous says it well, "I believe that the pain I feel by remembering cannot be any worse than the pain I feel by knowing and not remembering."

PRAYER

Compassionate one,
I believe your Holy Spirit has a two-edged sword —
with one side you reveal,
and with the other side you heal.
You read my thoughts and know my heart,
please reveal truth to me.
Free me from any deceit
causing me to walk in darkness.
Give me courage
to honestly confront the truth in my relationships.
Grant me strength to overcome fear
and walk in the light.
Open my eyes to see reality.
Open my ears to hear truth.
Open my mind to understand the steps
that lead to wholeness.
I desire to know the truth
so the truth can set me free.
I have come to believe
that you are the way and the truth and the life.
Please teach me truth in my heart.
Let me no longer seek
to hide from myself and from you.

AMEN.

CHAPTER TWO

Rejection

"My God, my God, why have you deserted me?" (Ps 22). I have often pondered these words uttered by Jesus Christ. With his last breath he is crying out feelings of abandonment, loss, and rejection. His sense of being disconnected from God, from his disciples, from his mother seems to be exceedingly painful.

The physical body of Jesus is wracked with pain. Yet he is not screaming about this torture. His words reflect the greater torment of being emotionally separated. The feelings of being rejected and cut off appear to cause him great grief.

Feelings of rejection associated with broken relationships are a devastating component of divorce trauma. A sense of not being wanted, a blow to self-esteem, a belief that one is no longer desirable all contribute to the rejection response. "The person who vowed to remain with me forever no longer wants our relationship," we think. Even if you are the one initiating the divorce, this sense of abandonment is often a strong emotional factor.

The human heart was created for connectedness, as is so beautifully demonstrated by the verses of the Song of Songs. "Come then, my love, my lovely one, come. For see, winter is past, the rains are over and gone. . . . Show me your face, let me hear your voice; for your voice is sweet and your face is beautiful" (Sg 2:10-11, 14).

The words of most popular love songs also attest to our need for connection. Many movies and television shows portray the drama and heartache of human relatedness. Union with another is a subject that never seems to be exhausted. Longing for harmonious relationships is the continuing quest of male/female psychology and the human condition.

Marriage supposedly puts an end to this longing. At last there is someone whose love for you will never die. Facing the reality of failure when the relationship is no longer life-giving is often so painful that many couples choose to ignore the obvious. Many live in a kind of silent divorce avoiding confrontation with the truth and postponing the possible consequences.

In my own life, I was well aware that the marital relationship was over for years before I could admit to it. But I still refused to believe my spouse and I no longer wanted to be together. I worked hard at being indispensable by taking care of the domestic and financial details that my husband disliked doing. Most people see me as a self-confident woman, observing me speaking before large gatherings or leading healing services for hundreds of people. I work hard at making a positive impression since my inner self is very sensitive to rejection and criticism. I am a perfectionist about doing things well and looking good.

Many factors compelled me to cease denying the truth. When the pain became greater than the fear of facing rejection and criticism, I finally admitted I was finished. The first time I said, "he no longer wants me," it was the most devastating reality I had ever faced. Even now, when I repeat the phrase, I experience overwhelming fear. Asking myself why this happened brings little relief because the feelings of abandonment remain. Writing out a list of all the differences between us helped my mind to comprehend the inevitability of separation, but my heart still felt unacceptable and undesirable.

While some forms of self-affirmation, such as looking in the mirror and saying, "I am a loveable and worthwhile person," can be somewhat helpful, they fall short of bringing comfort to a broken heart. Generally it is too difficult to be objective enough to confidently accept the words being said. Other attempts at self-affirmation, such as immediately establishing an emotional/sexual liaison with another to prove one's desirability and self-worth usually prove disastrous.

Finding a divorce recovery group or making a healing retreat can often provide a milieu for facing the pain of rejection. Allowing others to affirm and point out special qualities of your personality can begin to soften the blow of rejection. One method of accomplishing this is to ask close friends and family members to share a meaningful character trait they observe in you. Many people are often pleasantly surprised by the feedback of this exercise.

Regaining a sense of self-worth is a slow process. Indeed, it may be one of the hardest areas to heal. The heart, the most sensitive part of the inner self, has been wounded deeply. It has experienced so much pain that the journey toward recovery may seem endless.

In addition to a sense of rejection on the human level, a divorced person often experiences feelings of being emotionally and spiritually rejected by God. The sense of being separated from the creator is a response to strong feelings of abandonment. The heart cries out, "Why have you forsaken me when you promised to never leave me?"

Christian spirituality can provide help for the seemingly hopeless devastation of rejection. The Bible constantly gives reminders of the Father's everlasting love, compassion, and caring. "Does a woman forget her baby at the breast, or fail to cherish the son of her womb? Yet even if these forget, I will never forget you," says the Lord (Is 49:15). The scriptures are filled with promises regarding the willingness of God to remain close to his people even when all seems to be lost. Reading stories such as the Prodigal Son and the Woman at the Well may provide a more balanced perception of the situation.

Finding quiet moments throughout the day to *just sit in the presence of the one who loves unconditionally* can console the ravages of rejection. "A belief system which trusts in God seems to greatly enhance the healing process following divorce," stated one therapist who deals exclusively with family counseling. This is especially true where overwhelming feelings of abandonment have been experienced. The healing love of God is available as we cry out for his assistance.

PRAYER

Jesus, you experienced
the pain of being rejected.
Thus you understand my heart's sadness
at feeling cast aside and abandoned
by the one who vowed to love me.
I am overwhelmed
by a sense of disconnectedness.
I am frightened by feelings of abandonment.
Sometimes I even feel separated from God.
I no longer believe
I am a precious person.
Please take note of my despair
and grant me the touch of your consolation.

> *"He will not break the crushed reed,*
> *nor put out the smoldering wick*
> *till he has led the truth to victory:*
> *in his name the nations*
> *will put their hope"* (Mt 12:20-21).

Let me hear words of affirmation
reminding me of my goodness.
Bring others into my life
who can assist me with the restoration of self worth.
I trust in your ability
to heal my wounded heart.
Help me to be patient
while I wait for the fulfillment of your promises.

AMEN.

CHAPTER THREE

Fear

Feelings of fear crept over me like a suffocating blanket. I could be walking in the mall, driving down the highway, or talking with a friend and suddenly become gripped with terrifying anxiety. The palms of my hands would begin to sweat, my heart would race, my chest felt tight and I became light-headed.

The frequency and duration of these panic attacks made me believe that I was physically ill. However, subsequent medical tests did not substantiate my diagnosis. "Have you recently been experiencing unusual amounts of stress?" inquired the examining physician. "Yes, doctor, I'm going through a divorce." He explained the current research data that unquestionably places divorce at the *top* of the stress scale.

Psychosomatic illnesses, the wear and tear of the mind and emotions on the physical body, affects approximately 90% of the patients seen in a physician's practice. This information is not foreign to me since I have been a registered nurse for more than thirty years. Yet, understanding the phenomena did not lessen my attacks. Fear continued to hound my waking hours and disrupt my sleep at night.

So I decided to dialogue with the feelings. "What are you afraid of?" I asked myself. The answers flooded my thinking. The list of named fears, rational and irrational, filled two notebook pages.

Since I had always considered myself somewhat fearless in meeting the challenges life had to offer, this came as a huge shock. Wasn't I usually the one who functioned best during crises and who seldom lost composure in the most chaotic situations? Panic attacks were never an occurrence in my life and enduring feelings of fear was a completely new sensation for my nervous system and psyche to handle.

Topping my list was, "The fear of feeling fearful." I was afraid of feeling afraid. Such a reaction seems crazy and irrational and so it is. Feelings are not rational, not subject to reason. They arise from the unconscious part of the mind and are neither right nor wrong, good nor bad. They simply *are*. Feelings keep us in touch with our humanity because they remind the physical body that it is connected with the mind and spirit.

Feelings have a lot of energy attached to them, especially those that aren't given much attention or aren't processed in healthy ways. If we repress certain feelings into the deep unconscious, giving them only fleeting entry to our conscious awareness, they can pack quite a wallop when they begin to emerge.

Fear was such an emotion for me, a completely unknown entity in my emotional framework. Perhaps this conditioning resulted from childhood memories of my mother's frequent comment, "That child has no fear." I would hang from tree limbs or perform other such death-defying acts as a young child. As an adult, however, the stress associated with divorce threw my inner being into such chaos that I could no longer disregard fear. My ordinary coping mechanisms proved useless. Years of denial caused this reservoir of fearful feelings to shift into overdrive, flooding every part of me.

Feelings can throw the central nervous system into turmoil, but much can be done to redirect these emotions into healthier channels. My first task was to admit to myself and to at least one other person what I was afraid of. It's important to put a name on the fear and to clearly state what it is. "I am afraid of the future," or "I am afraid of losing my friends," etc. We cannot effectively deal with fear until it has a name and no longer remains some nebulous, free-floating feeling.

Initially it was unbelievably difficult for me to articulate my fears, but I persisted in talking to my friends about these heretofore unexperienced feelings. Verbalizing the fears carried in my heart helped me to better recognize the physical symptoms associated with the emotions of fear. I became less afraid of being afraid.

Then I found it necessary to differentiate the valid from the invalid fears. My fears concerning the necessities of life, i.e., where to live, how to support myself, what would happen to my relationship with the children, were all important considerations for the future. But they could only be addressed one at a time. I had to choose the most important area of concern facing me and deal with it until some type of resolution was attained. Facing one fear at a time kept me from going into emotional overload. I learned to turn off my panic attacks by doing something constructive to prove that I wasn't totally powerless over everything in my life. For example, I began looking at my talents and abilities to see what type of work was best suited for me. I soon realized that there were areas of possibilities to be pursued regarding my career.

The invalid fears were feelings of damnation, being cut off from God, losing eternal life. Verbalizing these feelings to at least one other person greatly reduced their power. I was fortunate to have a wonderful therapist who helped me sort out these levels of fear. I urge anyone severely impaired by nameless terror to find a counselor to be a mediator of peace.

I also discovered that many of the irrational fears could be abated by calling upon the merciful love of the Lord and prayerfully admitting my feelings to him.

PRAYER

Dear Lord,
I am so afraid.
What will become of me?
Is there still life to be lived
after this time of chaos?
Fear grips my entire being.
Sometimes I dream of being annihilated
and I awaken drenched in sweat.
The words of the psalmist
become my constant refrain:

> *My God, my God, why have you deserted me? . . .*
> *I call all day, my God, but you never answer,*
> *all night long I call and cannot rest . . . .*
> *Do not stand aside: trouble is near,*
> *I have no one to help me! (Ps 22:1-2, 11).*

Creator of my being,
I am terrified.

My deepest terror
is the fear of losing eternal life.
My salvation seems in jeopardy.
I fear you have turned your back on me.
Yet, I believe you are with me
in these dark moments.
In the first letter of John, Jesus taught us,

> *"In love there can be no fear,*
> *but fear is driven out by perfect love:*
> *because to fear is to expect punishment,*
> *and anyone who is afraid*
> *is still imperfect in love"* (1 Jn 4:18).

I cling to these words like a life preserver.
My feelings of fear
have nothing to do with your actions.
In the midst of my fears
you are still there.
Thank you for never abandoning me.
Thank you for never letting go of my hand.
Together we walk through this frightening time
of doubt and uncertainty
as I again hear your words,

> *"There is no need to be afraid*
> *. . . for it has pleased your Father*
> *to give you the kingdom"* (Lk 12:32).

AMEN.

CHAPTER FOUR

Grief

Grief is a word normally used to describe the feelings associated with the loss of a loved one through death. There was no physical death in the relationship between me and my former spouse, yet during the weeks and months following the divorce, my heart seemed filled with much sadness. I cried often; it seemed to require very little stimuli to produce copious tears.

One day I found some old photos from early in our marriage. We looked happy and peaceful. We were together for life! Divorce was not an option. But the non-option became a reality. Sorrow brought a constant lump in my throat, I felt a heaviness in my chest. My reddened and swollen eyes made reading difficult so I spent many hours staring out the window, blindly watching the TV screen or walking aimlessly through the shopping mall.

Ordinarily I was very active, even attending aerobics class three times weekly. But the devastation wrought by the divorce made dusting the furniture seem strenuous. I had to force myself to take a shower and get dressed.

Often the telephone would ring but I avoided answering it, preferring to let the caller talk to my machine. I seldom returned the calls. It took too much energy to talk. There seemed to be an invisible shield between me and the rest of the world. I was alone on an island. Often visions of a cemetery or tombstones entered my nightly dreams.

I now recognize this behavior as my response to intense grief. The breakup of a marriage is a loss like the death of a spouse. All the emotions associated with grief — sorrow, pining, yearning, denial, despair — are an intense part of the divorce syndrome. But there are some important distinctions. Divorce evokes more anger than death because it is, seemingly, more optional. Guilt and self-reproach are generally stronger. Feelings of abandonment can be even more intense, "He didn't have to leave me."

According to recent studies, the physical and emotional costs of divorce can be higher than those imposed by a spouse's death. Many divorcees state they would rather be widowed because death does not carry the social stigma nor entangle them in continuing fights over property and children. Nor does it often cause the strong feelings of failure generated by divorce.

The loss of a mate with whom we have shared a history shatters the former conditions of our life. Grief is a normal and indeed necessary part of the recovery process. Mourning is triggered by our regrets regarding the termination of the marriage. We grieve the loss of expectations, the loss of dreams for the future. Giving up the hope of spending our "golden years" in quiet simplicity was excruciatingly painful for me. To no longer contemplate sharing the joys of grandparenthood still prompts overwhelming sorrow.

Every time I considered the effect of divorce on our five grown children, it filled me with unbearable remorse. Although they were not embroiled in the bitter custody battle of dependent children, they *were* being emotionally torn by their parents' breakup. Our decision to separate meant selling the family home. We no longer would have a place to gather for holidays, weddings, and birthdays. Causing emotional suffering to the ones we love the most was the deepest form of grief for me. I remember praying to die rather than bring them pain. Learning to allow the children to process and resolve grief in their own way was not an easy task for me. I found it important to make a distinction between my sadness and their sorrow in order to effectively handle my own grief issues. (In Chapter Eight I deal more fully with divorce and children.)

Losing the family home as a result of the divorce agreement was a great sorrow for all of us. I walked through the house remembering gatherings of happy times for holidays, birthdays, graduations, proms, weddings. We would no longer have a place to call home, a place that represented togetherness. After our divorce it took me a long time to be able to accept invitations to dinner at the home of married couples. The anguish of being in a real home was more than I could bear.

Dividing up the belongings produced a high degree of distress because a part of our history was contained in everything we owned. I would wander through the house aimlessly touching pieces of furniture and sobbing uncontrollably.

Separation shock is the term that best describes the grief syndrome associated with divorce. The termination of a relationship, no matter how long its duration, sends waves of depression and melancholy throughout our being. We go through the motions of living, but feel like the walking dead.

Divorce is a death. It must be treated with the same forms of grief reduction necessary for coping with physical death. The feelings associated with the mourning process need an outlet. Remaining in isolation, stuffing the feelings, resigning from the human race will not make it go away.

Refusing to deal with the sorrow will generally cause unhealthy coping mechanisms to develop. *If we don't deal with our feelings, our feelings deal with us.* Psychosomatic responses such as insomnia, diarrhea/constipation, shortness of breath, sexual disturbances, stress-related illness are not uncommon. Recent studies indicate the causative factor in the development of addictive behavior patterns is undiscovered/unexpressed/unresolved grief.

Recognizing the sorrow and misery accompanying separation and divorce, and employing suitable measures for grief reduction, can greatly assist this difficult time of passage. The importance of supportive friends who walk with us cannot be undervalued. The feelings associated with grief have much energy attached to them. Trying to deal with them "on our own" is self-defeating. There has to be at least one other person who can listen to my anguish so it doesn't stay stuck inside. My friend Linda spent many hours quietly listening to my cries of travail. She is a true reflection of the one Henri Nouwen describes:

> When we honestly ask ourselves which persons in our lives mean the most to us, we often find that it is those who, instead of giving much advice, solutions, or cures, have chosen rather to share our pain and touch our wounds with a gentle and tender hand. The friend who can be silent with us in a moment of despair or confusion, who can stay with us in an hour of grief and bereavement, who can tolerate not knowing, not curing, not healing and

and face with us the reality of our powerlessness, that is the friend who cares.[1]

If we have no such person in our lives, we can ask Jesus, the one who calls us friend, to send someone who can be a source of comfort or to help us find a grief support group. Sometimes "[we] don't have what [we] want . . . because [we] don't pray for it" (Jas 4:2).

Many churches and community mental health programs provide support groups for divorced and separated persons. The old adage, "just give it time," is faulty thinking regarding the grief process. People often wait around for years with the idea that after a long enough period of time they will feel better again. Isolation and withdrawal from the world only add to our already overloaded sense of sadness.

The Twelve Step program that emerged from Alcoholics Anonymous also is an exceptionally valuable tool for dealing with grief. Groups such as Codependents Anonymous and Adult Children of Alcoholics can provide a framework of non-judgmental, loving, listening companions to help in our journey toward wellness. We don't have to remain forever stuck in this pain.

Another helpful method of dealing with grief involves ritualizing the experience. When someone dies, we go through a wake and funeral to give outward expression to our sorrow. It provides some sense of closure and of letting go of the relationship. One couple told me they respectfully returned the wedding rings to one another to symbolize the ending of the relationship. Such a gesture is not appropriate or desirable in many cases but there can be other forms of rituals. Members of some Native American tribes offer an interesting example. When a person experiences an overwhelming sense of grief, she goes into the woods and digs a hole and symbolically places the pain back into the earth where it can regenerate and give life again. Perhaps such rituals seem strange, but our hearts cry out for a way to externalize the grief and bring meaning into it.

Part of my grief reduction involved taking my gold wedding band and having it reset with a beautiful opal, the gem of fidelity, prayers, and assurance. Leaving it at the jewelers yielded many tears but assisted me in getting in touch with some of the more hidden areas of grief.

It takes time to go through this valley of tears and, no matter how hard we try, we cannot rush the process. Because each person responds to grief differently, it can be self-defeating to compare our recovery rate to that of another. The fact that my recently divorced friend seems to be advancing in recovery faster than me, doesn't mean I'm a failure.

It is not a sign of defeat if we find it necessary to seek professional counseling to assist this process. The wise person avails herself of all possible remedies in the pursuit of wholeness. This is especially true if we remain stuck in grief, unable to let go of the past. Many avenues of recovery are available for those who choose to live again after the sorrow of separation.

Ernest Hemingway wrote, "The world breaks everyone, and, afterwards some are stronger in the broken places." Some become stronger and some do not — the choice is ours. The pain of divorce can be a means to deeper psychological/spiritual growth if we discover healthy ways to recognize and integrate these feelings.

As Christians we can invite God to bring comfort into this time of sadness. The scriptures promise, "Happy those who mourn: they shall be comforted" (Mt 5:5).

PRAYER

Compassionate friend,
in the Garden of Olives you cried,
"My soul is sorrowful
to the point of death . . ." (Mt 26:38).
You are no stranger to grief.
My heart too is overcome with sadness.
I mourn for the loss
of the love relationship
with my former spouse.
I cry for the shattered dreams.
My heart aches when contemplating
the unrealized hopes and uncompleted plans
that are no longer possible.
Broken promises
and betrayal of trust
bring agony into my heart.
Sometimes the pain is so overwhelming
I no longer want to live.
The words of Psalm 6 echo within me,
"I have no strength left . . .
my bones are in torment . . .
I am worn out with groaning,
every night I drench my pillow
and soak my bed with tears;
my eye is wasted with grief."

Lord, comfort me in my sorrow.
Let me feel your gentle arms
surrounding my tired body.
Give me your strength so I may continue
the passage through this time of sadness.

Jesus, my friend,
I believe you cry with me
just as you cried with Martha and Mary
over the death of their brother, Lazarus.
Your love is there to sustain me
even when I fail to feel it.
Guide me to discover persons in my life
who can reflect your compassion.
Grant me courage
to reconnect with others
and discover healing as I share the depths of my grief
with those who hear my cry for help.
In your mercy I ask you to exchange
"for ashes a garland;
for mourning robe the oil of gladness,
for despondency, praise . . ." (Is 61:3).

AMEN.

CHAPTER FIVE

Anger

It's hard not to be angry over this turn of events in my life. I tried to lead a good Christian life and, to the best of my ability, followed the teachings of the gospel. Under the guidance of the Holy Spirit, I accepted the call to minister and saw the hand of God work many healings during two decades of Christian service.

Why wasn't my marriage healed? I prayed for countless others having marital discord and many were reconciled. Yet the relationship between Ben and I continued to deteriorate. We sought counseling, had the best of spiritual direction, spent hours in prayer, and became even more estranged from each other.

My anger was primarily directed at God. Along with St. Teresa of Avila I cried, "If this is how you treat your friends, no wonder you have so few." Where was my all-loving, compassionate creator? Was this a form of punishment for some sin in my life? My prayer became a constant plea for his mercy, "Please, I beg you to heal this marriage."

Bible accounts of those who lashed out in anger toward God gave me some consolation. Moses is a prime example:

> Moses heard the people wailing, every family at
> the door of its tent. . . . And he spoke to Yahweh:
> "Why do you treat your servant so badly? Why
> have I not found favor with you, so that you load
> on me the weight of all this nation? The weight is
> too much for me. If this is how you want to deal
> with me, I would rather you killed me! If only I had
> found favor in your eyes, and not lived to see such
> misery as this!" (Nm 11:10-11, 14-15).

The Lord did not reprimand Moses for his outburst. Instead he seemed to commend this direct communication by telling him to "Gather seventy of the elders of Israel... [and] bring them to the Tent of Meeting. . . . I will take some of the spirit which is on you and put it on them. So they will share with you the burden of this nation, and you will no longer have to carry it by yourself" (Nm 11:16-17).

As long as Moses tried to "stuff" his feelings of anger and pretend they didn't exist, Yahweh did nothing to relieve his misery. Reading these passages gave me courage to confront my own anger toward the God of my creation. Often I would drive to the beach near my home in Florida, walk to an isolated area and scream out my frustrations. The Lord of the universe did not seem to recoil from my outbursts and this helped to take the edge off my emotional overload.

Feelings of anger have tremendous amounts of energy attached to them. Sooner or later it will show itself. Particularly if it is intense or of long standing duration, it will find an outlet. Anger can lead to a variety of debilitating physical symptoms and illnesses. Ulcers, tension headaches, skin disorders (hives, eczema, rashes), asthma, colitis, are but a few examples of anger-related conditions. The body was not meant to store anger and, eventually, it rebels.

> Anger can be an enemy, damaging bodies, disrupting relationships, destroying families and communities. Or it can be a friend. If we learn to recognize the physiological and psychological signs that accompany anger, it will be less likely to slip unnoticed and unintended into our behavior. Rather it will serve as a beacon of self-knowledge and an energy source for action. Examining the things that evoke anger in us can tell something about the kinds of needs we have. It can lead us to review our life. It can help us to name the barriers to our needs and to come to know whether those barriers are real or imagined, old or new, erected by circumstances beyond our control or erected unnecessarily by ourselves.[2]

Knowing I was angry and learning to recognize the symptoms of stored anger put me in the position of taking charge of my anger instead of it taking charge of me.

Ben and I were angry at one another, but we seldom verbalized it. Instead we chose to avoid each other as much as possible and find ways to direct the anger energy into physical activities. However, my thoughts toward him were anything but generous. Bitterness was finding a way into my heart.

I was falling into a habit of thinking common among divorced persons — finger-pointing and blaming. Often we are dissatisfied with ourselves, but failing to recognize this symptom, we project the anger outward onto the handiest target — the ex-spouse — and the gender he or she represents. We think, "All men are worthless!" or, "You can never trust a woman!"

Owning my self-dissatisfaction was a first step in resolving the overload of angry feelings. In truth, the most subtle form of anger and the most vicious was directed toward myself. My inner voice was constantly chastising, "You really messed up this time! You never do anything right!" I recalled previous failures in relationships and accused myself of being totally incapable of loving others.

Recognizing feelings of anger did not automatically assure mastery over this area. Dr. Harriet Goldhor Lerner writes:

> Jog, meditate, ventilate, bite your tongue, silently count to ten ... there is no shortage of advice about what you can do with anger in the short run. Some experts will tell you to get it out of your system as quickly as possible and others offer different advice. In the long run, however, it is not what you do or don't do with your anger at a particular moment that counts. The important issue is whether, over time, you can use your anger as an incentive to achieve greater self-clarity and discover new ways to navigate old relationships. *Anger gets us nowhere if we unwittingly perpetuate the old patterns from which our anger springs.*[3]

To discover unhealthy methods of approaching anger, it was necessary to overcome the belief learned in my formative years (in home and in school): anger is wrong, bad, unacceptable and unladylike. I had to teach my inner self that anger is a healthy, important and life-giving feeling.

It took me a bit of work to identify my personal pattern of dealing with anger in order to become more effective with this emotion. My pattern goes somewhat like this: I am very much afraid of another's anger and generally succeed in avoiding those who have a short fuse. When anger rises within, I shut down my feelings, stop communicating and distance myself (emotionally and physically) from the person who aroused the reaction. Often this is accompanied by feelings of much tiredness and fatigue.

I am learning to step back and observe myself when things get hot. I try to stay in the situation and find ways to admit my feelings. The first time I said, "I am feeling angry" to another person was a big step toward wholeness.

I now know feelings of anger are an appropriate response to the trauma of divorce. When the entire course of one's life is re-directed with the rupture of a primary relationship, becoming angry is a sign of emotional health! However, giving reign to these feelings through rage and violence is not acceptable.

Following our separation, I continued to cry out angrily to God over his apparent lack of concern for our marriage. I accepted an invitation to lead a group of pilgrims to Rome, Yugoslavia, and the Holy Land. My intention was to plead for reconciliation of our marriage in all the holy places. For an hour one Saturday evening in the church of St. James in Medjugorje, I poured out my heart to God. "Why aren't you healing my marriage?" I demanded over and over again. Then the room became very still. Despite the many hundreds of people, I felt alone with the Lord. Very distinctly, in the core of my being, I heard the words, "I cannot heal what never was." It came like an arrow into my heart. This was a concept I never understood. Healing means restoration, a return to a former state of wholeness. Our marriage couldn't be healed because it never was a total union of love. From the beginning it lacked the components of the two becoming one flesh. My anger at God's seeming indifference finally brought about the answer. As I knelt in the darkened church, a number of priests were moving through the crowd, blessing the people with holy oil. An elderly priest walked over to me, made the sign of the cross on my forehead and said, "The Lord is opening a new door for you. Don't be afraid to walk through it." After my return from the pilgrimage I shared this insight with Ben and we then agreed to proceed with the divorce.

St. Paul understood the human experience of anger, but in his letter to the Ephesians, he gives some clear guidelines on managing this powerful emotion. His advice is beneficial to all who are facing the agony of divorce and separation. The healthy use of anger energy can be an important companion in the process of recovery. There is no morality to the feeling of anger. However, the behavior associated with angry feelings is always to be avoided.

> Even if you are angry, you must not sin: never let the sun set on your anger or else you will give the devil a foothold . . . never have grudges against others, or lose your temper, or raise your voice to anybody, or call each other names, or allow any sort of spitefulness (Eph 4:26-27, 31).

PRAYER

Lord, my heart is full of anger
over the dissolution of my marriage.
I am beginning to identify
angry feelings toward you, my God.
Why do you ignore my pleas for healing?
Why do you disregard my cries for help?
You are a God of love,
yet you demonstrate no love toward me
as I beg for your assistance.
Perhaps you are testing my faith
but I am weary of believing that you care.

"I cry to you, and you give me no answer;
I stand before you, but you take no notice.
You have grown cruel in your dealings with me,
your hand lies on me, heavy and hostile" (Jb 30:20-21).

I also feel bitterness
toward my ex-spouse for this misery.
I want to lash out,
to wound with words and actions
the one who was once my lover.
When I finally quiet the raging torrent of my mind
and listen to the voices within,
I am aware of feelings of anger toward myself.
Words of accusation flood my heart.
The blame I outwardly acknowledge
is a form of antagonism against my own being.
Self-dissatisfaction threatens to consume me.

Lord, I believe you do not desert me
even when I express these angry feelings.
You created me with an ability
to experience passionate emotions.
Help me direct the energy generated by my anger
into suitable channels of life.
Let me not use this powerful resource
for destructive purposes.
Rather, let it give strength
to move me to resolve the important issues
of my present life.

"God, examine me and know my heart,
probe me and know my thoughts;
make sure I do not follow pernicious ways,
and guide me in the way that is everlasting"
(Ps 139:23-24).

AMEN.

CHAPTER SIX

Shame

It sometimes seemed I would never feel happiness again. The constant sense of condemnation never ceased to haunt me, in spite of attempts at confession and self-affirmation.

I repeated to myself positive scripture verses from the book of Isaiah, "I have called you by your name, you are mine . . . you are precious in my eyes" (43:1, 4). I practiced saying affirming statements like, "You are a worthwhile and loveable woman," but all to no avail.

The answer to this dilemma came in the form of a cassette tape entitled, "Barbara, This Is Your Life," sent by my dear friend, Fr. Jack McGinnis. For several days I avoided listening to it, afraid to believe it would be beneficial. "Jack doesn't know the real me," I rationalized. "If he did he couldn't say anything positive about my life."

Finally, in desperation one night when I was overwhelmed with a sense of despair, I played the tape.

It contained ninety minutes of Jack's sharing of detailed situations when I influenced his priesthood and brought healing into his heart during the nearly fifteen years of our friendship. The narrative was interspersed with some of Jack's original music which spoke of God's tenderness toward his children. The wall of defenses around my heart started to crack ever so slightly as I accepted the truth of Jack's statement, "You are loved and loveable."

Each time I listened to his words, the sense of condemnation lessened a little more. Affirmation really took root when I heard it from another human person. Self-affirmation can be helpful, but the human heart cries out to hear these words from others, especially when the trauma of divorce threatens to completely undermine self-worth. My inner being started to heal when I gave myself permission to accept the truth of Jack's statements.

This experience gave me insight concerning the difference between guilt and shame. Guilt is an action word — it's about the things I do that offend God, other people, or myself. The Holy Spirit comes into my heart, convicting me of these wrongs, inviting me to repentance and behavioral changes. When I am guilty of a transgression, something can be done about it.

But the accusatory words I was hearing in my head were not convicting me of specific sins that I could confess and receive forgiveness for. These words made me feel like a complete waste. They were condemning me by saying, "You're no good. You never do anything right. Your salvation is lost." The light finally dawned: I was dealing with *shame*. Shame is an excruciatingly internal experience of exposure. It gives rise to feelings of being unprotected, naked, and ugly.

This explained my inability to overcome the inner voices. I was approaching them in the wrong way. I was trying to repent for my feelings of being flawed. Guilt is about breaking rules. It says, "I made a mistake," and the proper response is, "I'm sorry." Shame is about feeling bad and it says, "I am a mistake." The proper response is to get out from under it.

Learning about shame and its subtle invasion of my soul has been a profound spiritual experience for me. I began to recognize "shame attacks" when they occurred. When someone criticizes me or rejects me, I experience a complete shut-down of feelings. This state of numbness, this feeling of being a "wart on the face of society" used to persist for several days. Self-hatred was a constant companion.

Others have described "shame attacks" characterized by feelings of dizziness, nausea, light-headedness. Fr. Jack says he experiences a huge ball of fire in his abdomen during such episodes. These physical symptoms are usually coupled with thoughts of worthlessness, a sense of failing and falling short as a human being. John Bradshaw in his book *Healing the Shame That Binds You* describes shame as a rupture of the self with the self. He further states, "It is like internal bleeding. A shame-based person will guard against exposing his inner self to others, but more significantly, he will guard against exposing himself to himself. There is shame about shame."[4]

Until Bradshaw raised consciousness about shame, it was not considered an important emotion. I can remember hearing many sermons about guilt and the importance of repentance, but only recently is the Christian community focusing attention on this neglected area of psycho/spiritual development.

I was greatly relieved to be able to identify and name this phenomena in my own life. In order to discern the difference between guilt and shame, I ask myself, "What rule did I break?" If no answer is forthcoming, I am learning to adopt various shame-reduction techniques to alleviate the symptoms. Admitting to myself and to others, "I feel a sense of shame about _____," is a big step. This acknowledgment takes the emotion out of the shadows where it prefers to remain and brings it into the light so I can deal with it.

Often I dialogue with the feeling to discover what triggered the sense of being flawed. Recently I was giving a weekend retreat to a group of women and I began experiencing a sense of discomfort and embarrassment. During the coffee break I went back to my room and talked to myself. "When did you start feeling this way?" The answer came as I recalled an earlier conversation with one of the participants. She mentioned seeing me on a recent television presentation, "You looked sort of washed out. Perhaps you need someone to help you with your makeup," she remarked. She pushed the button for a shame attack and my inner self was sending out the signals. Recognizing this emotional trigger gave me insight to work with the feelings and not become overwhelmed. The feelings of embarrassment were lessened when I returned to the group and said, "I'm looking for someone to teach me the art of makeup so I won't look washed out on video." Everyone laughed and so did I.

Most persons suffer acute feelings of shame following a marital breakup, especially if they have strong religious beliefs against divorce. We are often haunted by a sense of being defective. "There must be something wrong with me or I would still be in the marriage," is a common form of thinking. We may feel extreme self-disgust and self-hatred.

Fossum and Mason, the authors of *Facing Shame* write, "A person with guilt might say, 'I feel awful seeing that I did something which violated my values.'"[5] In so doing the person's values are reaffirmed. The possibility of repair exists and learning and growth are promoted. While guilt is a painful feeling of regret and responsibility for one's actions, shame is a painful feeling about oneself as a person. The possibility of repair seems foreclosed to the shameful person because shame is a matter of identity, not of behavioral infraction. There is nothing to be learned from it and no growth is opened by the experience because it only confirms one's negative feelings about oneself.

I found it very important in the early stages of divorce recovery to surround myself with loving persons and, to the best of my ability, to avoid those who emotionally kicked me. Most areas of the country have self-help groups, Twelve Step programs, or meetings for the divorced and separated that provide a safe environment for further growth. The word *safe* is a key factor. The group must be non-judgmental and non-shaming. A person who feels unduly exposed by the words or actions of group leaders or other participants is probably not going to make much progress toward overcoming shame.

Identifying and expressing the strong emotions connected to shame is not easy. It is best to go slowly and to try not to rush the process. At first it feels strange and scary even to admit the existence of personal shame. However, just to be able to put a name to it is often the most effective form of shame reduction.

The Bible can also provide comfort from the strangle hold of this emotion. "Every face turned to him grows brighter and is never ashamed," the psalmist proclaims (Ps 34:5). Throughout the New Testament we read stories of Jesus befriending and healing those considered outcast and untouchable in the Jewish community. The lepers, prostitutes, and tax collectors discovered renewed self-esteem through the touch of the healer.

My prayer time ceased being a stand-off between me and the Lord as I stopped begging God to forgive me for being flawed. Like St. Paul, I now proclaim, "those who are in Christ Jesus are not condemned, [because] the law of the spirit of life in Christ Jesus has set you free from the law of sin and death" (Rom 8:1-2). Those who believe in divine mercy now walk in the light of his redeeming love.

The one who redeemed me has already freed me from the chains of self-loathing. "For the sake of the joy which was still in the future, he endured the cross, disregarding the shamefulness of it, and from now on has taken his place at the right of God's throne" (Heb 12:2). I can invite God to heal the roots of shame within me as I come to recognize and resolve this hold on my life.

PRAYER

O merciful one,
feelings of judgment
and damnation
flood my soul.
I am engulfed
by a sense of shame
that tells me
I am ugly, flawed, and defiled.
Many experiences
during my journey through life
have given rise
to feelings of shame.
Abusive words and actions
toward me
have spoken lies to my heart.
Separation and divorce
add fuel to this fire
and a sense of unworthiness
overwhelms me.
I am powerless
over the waves of shame
attacking my inner self.

I believe your grace
is made perfect in my weakness.
I call upon your strength
to overcome my affliction.
Heal the memories
associated with emotional pain
and liberate me
from all self-hatred.
Help me trust
in your gift of unconditional love
which disregards
my faults and failures.
Grant me friendships
that mirror your affirmation of my being.
I accept the mercy
coming from your heart into mine, for
 "if the Son makes you free,
you will be free indeed" (Jn 8:36).

AMEN.

CHAPTER SEVEN

Guilt

My head is filled with "if only" thoughts today. If only we had tried harder. If only I had been more loving. If only I had been more understanding. This unending list carries a consistent message of condemnation: I really messed up! It's all my fault. I made a mistake.

As a lifelong Roman Catholic I was taught the evils of divorce and the severe punishment awaiting those who did not remain true to their vows. A conversation with a priest friend promised to enlighten my darkened soul. "The Catholic church is starting to take a more compassionate look at the sacrament of matrimony. At one time the phrase 'till death do us part' in the marriage ceremony referred to actual physical death. Now many church leaders are saying it can also apply to the *death of the relationship.*" The phrase *death of a relationship* resonated within me. When marriage partners no longer bring life to one another and, in fact, present barriers for growth, then psychological divorce has already occurred. For many years such symptoms were obvious in my marriage. But a dogged determination to succeed kept us trying to make it work. Trying harder proved exhausting and fruitless.

My guilty feelings were also triggered by the erroneous belief that a divorced person is excommunicated from the church and could no longer receive the sacraments. Discussing this misconception with a priest gave me a better understanding of the current teaching on the subject. Although becoming educated about these changes was helpful for my mind, still the feelings of guilt and condemnation persisted in my heart. It was the Lenten season, a time of preparation for the celebration of Easter and the victory of Jesus over the powers of darkness. All the readings during church services and in my daily prayer meditations were concentrated on the passion and agony of our Lord's final days on earth. It was not difficult to empathize with his pain as I sat in the back of the church weeping for my sins.

Sin is not a word generally heard in today's culture. It has a sense of condemnation attached to it. Contemplating transgressions is very uncomfortable and most of us avoid reflecting on our shortcomings. Sin in the truest definition of the word is a *refusal to love*. Someone is hurt or offended by my actions. The Hebrew concept of "missing the mark" probably describes it best. Sin means to misdirect our behavior in a way that fails to hit the bull's eye of honesty, truth, and love. We go astray and thus cause hurt and pain to ourselves or to others.

All major religions provide a time for introspection, time to take a moral inventory and turn the spotlight on self-evaluation. In the Jewish calendar the high holy days in the early fall conclude with the Day of Atonement. The mood of this day is contrite and sober because the gulf between what we are and what we ought to be highlights the need for repentance.

Repentance means to turn around, to be willing to change, to turn back to God. Guilt concerning our human frailty can be relieved when we admit weaknesses and seek God's mercy. Initially, there must be a conscious awareness of having missed the mark where love is concerned. This is not a time for rationalizations or excuses. It takes courage to acknowledge the truth concerning unkind or abusive actions and behavior.

It is very important that we differentiate between shame and guilt because we often confuse the two. Shame is a feeling of being bad. This sense of being flawed makes us feel miserable and unworthy. Conversely, guilt is an important and necessary component of a healthy personality. Whenever I break a rule, commit a transgression, or wound another, my conscience reminds me that I've strayed off the path and am missing the mark. My inner being is telling me that amends must be made to correct this problem. A person with no conscience, i.e., a psychopath, has a severe psychological problem because he is never aware that his harmful actions are causing pain and chaos to those around him.

Ordinarily we can discern whether or not a sense of discomfort is derived from guilt or shame by asking a few questions, "What rule did I break?" "Do I need to say I'm sorry?" "Is there some type if restitution I should make?"

The next step is equally difficult because it involves admitting our wrongdoings. Some Christian religions teach that it is not necessary *to confess* to another human person, but I have found it essential in the resolution of my own guilty feelings. It's interesting to note that the very successful format of Alcoholics Anonymous and all the subsequent Twelve Step programs, stresses the importance of openly sharing indiscretions with another person.

Step Four directs the individual to "make a searching and fearless moral inventory of themselves." Step Five says it is necessary "to admit to God, to ourselves, and to another human being the *exact* nature of our wrongs."

No matter what the circumstances of the divorce, no one was the total villain or the complete victim. Each spouse played a part in the drama and there were moments when the commandment to love one another was broken. Admitting these sins and seeking reconciliation with God is a big step toward relieving the guilt.

I found it helpful to sit quietly and write down the times I failed in loving my former spouse. This exercise did not increase my self-appreciation but did assist in uncovering a lot of unhealthy behavior.

During Holy Week I went to the sacrament of reconciliation, pouring out my heart by confessing all the faults and failures of my life. The priest was very gentle as he pronounced the ancient words of absolution over me. Then he added, "Barbara, you will continue to experience the dark night of the soul for a while. It is the soul's form of purification. For many years you have walked in the companionship of God and you have been a source of healing for a countless multitude of people. Will you continue to walk with the Lord without the comfort of feeling his closeness?" Softly whispering, "I'll try, Father," I went out into the darkened church to sit near the tabernacle and ponder his words.

Jesus said his blood was being shed for the forgiveness of sin; therefore, as soon as I admitted my wrongdoing, I was cleansed and washed of all defilement. The Bible said God forgave me, a priest had said, "Go, your sins are forgiven," yet, I found it most difficult to forgive myself.

I kept waiting to feel that sense of peace that previously marked union with my God. When it did not come, I was certain there was still more need for repentance. There was much I yet needed to learn about the feelings associated with separation and divorce. No magic cures or instant healings accompanied my search for freedom. Walking through this time of transition taught me to rely less on feelings of consolation and to walk by faith in the constant presence of the unseen one.

St. Gregory of Nyssa once declared, "The soul who is troubled is near unto God." The struggle and conflict of coming to grips with the changes in my life are not a sign of God's disfavor. Spiritual enlightenment occurs only when a person has been through the dark and disturbing trials of the soul, clinging to belief in his merciful love.

Learning to forgive myself is the greatest challenge of all, but, with the grace of God it can be done, one day at a time.

PRAYER

O faithful one,
please be with me
during this dark night of my soul.
I do not experience your tenderness
and I am not aware of your forgiveness.
There is a black hole inside me
that seems to absorb all your light.

> *"For I am well aware of my faults,*
> *I have my sin constantly in mind,*
> *having sinned against*
> *none other than you" (Ps 51:3-4).*

Grant me the courage
to admit my transgressions.
Help me to be honest about my sins.
Give me the grace
to confront my failings.

I throw myself upon your mercy.
I believe
"you will not scorn
this crushed and broken heart"(Ps 51:17).

Gentle Jesus,
help me
to be gentle with myself.
Grant me the grace
to forgive myself
for real or imagined sins.
Help me to trust
in your abiding love.
Give me strength
to remain in communion with you
 regardless of my feelings.
Help me to fight
my greatest enemy,
self-hatred and self-condemnation.
In faith,
I accept freedom
and thank you for forgiving me.

AMEN.

CHAPTER EIGHT

Children

Sigmund Freud once observed that being a parent is an impossible profession even under the best of circumstances. At no time does this statement hit closer to the truth than during the dissolution of a marriage. Parental fears concerning effects of divorce on the children is often their number one issue. No matter how destructive the marital relationship may be, most parents agonize over the disruption of the family unit. As one divorced man described it, "Telling our daughters that my wife and I were getting a divorce made me feel like a trapper clubbing baby seals." Indeed, finding ways to minimize the impact often becomes an obsession.

Divorce is almost always a traumatic experience for children and the effects of divorce appear to be long lasting. It is fortunate that more attention is now being given to studying the effects of divorce on children since one-half of Americans born in the 1980s will live in a one parent family before the age of eighteen. Their experience with fear, guilt, loss, and abandonment cannot be ignored or minimized.

The first months following separation generally find most children adding to the parents' mental dilemma by acting out their anger and distress in a variety of ways. The behavior may vary depending on the ages of the children, but it is usually calculated to punish the parents. "My kids have never been so unruly and disobedient. All I do is discipline them and it's driving me crazy," said one mother of three youngsters.

Dr. Diane Fassel states that the age of the child at the time of the divorce and the way it was handled has a decided effect on the child's emotional development.[6] Her research examined the lives of hundreds of adult children of divorce. Diane identified five types of divorce and their characteristics: the disappearing parent, the surprise divorce, the always fighting divorce, the let's-keep-this-from-the-kids divorce, and the late-in-life divorce. Each form of separation elicits a predictable reaction, depending on the age of the child.

Rocking the boat of family security causes a great deal of fear in the minds of children. Anger is a cover-up for fear and the child lashes out at the parent he or she feels *safest* in confronting. The parent who recognizes this to be a normal part of family divorce recovery will not get locked into false guilt and constant wrangling.

The mind and heart of a person undergoing the trauma of divorce is already overloaded with feelings of self-hatred and self-criticism. Therefore it becomes imperative not to accept the child's behavior at face value and believe, "I'm destroying her life, she will never get over this, I'm responsible for causing all this pain." It is true, the choices being made are affecting the child's lifestyle, but he or she is not the only one who is hurting.

Each person in the family is going through a time of pain, but since children are ordinarily more demonstrative, they may seem to be in greater turmoil. It is vital to keep in mind that emotional survival is possible for everyone, even when it seems to be impossible.

Our children were all adults at the time of the divorce, but the psychological trauma is still a factor in their lives. Each was living independent of us, all had completed their education, two were married. They are very close in age and we enjoyed much family togetherness during their growing up years. They never observed violent behavior between Ben and me, nor were there constant emotional outbursts of anger. In many ways our children were not prepared for the reality of a broken home.

It was deeply troubling for us to discuss how our decision would affect each one. The sale of the family home, the place where we gathered for holidays and special occasions, would be disturbing in many ways. I was particularly troubled as feelings of failure regarding the relationship consumed my waking hours. I was now exposed as a less-than-perfect parent and a fallible human being who made mistakes. I fully expected total rejection from all the children. I was certain they would forever hate me for not trying harder, for not loving their father, for not being a good Christian, for not living up to the values I taught them to have.

We chose a time when most of them could be together to break the news of our separation and possible divorce, but our oldest son was not able to be present. We explained that this was a mutual decision based on months of counseling, discussion, and prayer. They were understandably shaken and some of us were crying. The youngest son, David, spoke for all by stating, "We've been somewhat expecting this so it doesn't come as a complete surprise.

We've talked about it to each other and want you to know we love you both and will not take sides." It was a great relief to feel their love and concern, yet we both felt much regret for the pain being caused.

In the months following, they remained true to their promise and did not try to shut out either one of us while each processed their sorrow, disappointment, hurt, or anger in a different way. Often it was difficult to listen to their feelings and I had to work at not becoming defensive. I learned to say, "I'm sorry our separation is hurting you," without becoming overwhelmed with feelings of guilt and shame. It took a long time and I still have to work at it. My heart aches when I think about their pain. Many times I wished I could "put Humpty-Dumpty together again" and we could go back to the family we once seemed to be, but this is no longer possible.

Initially, we tried to pretend everything was still okay. Christmas arrived three months after we separated. Ben was in an apartment and I was still in the family home so I went about doing the usual holiday arrangements. As we gathered for the opening of presents and the traditional meal, the tension in the house seemed almost palpable. We were very polite to one another. Ben and I sat at the table like we always did but it felt phoney and unreal. We learned it was not possible to re-create our former togetherness, no matter how hard we tried.

The illusion of family was no longer honest and we would have to discover new ways of relating. Letting go of the traditions, especially during the holidays still continues to be a source of discomfort and sadness. Learning to share my vulnerability, fears, uncertainties, and sorrows with our adult children also remains a challenge for me. Less pretense and more honesty is not always comfortable and doesn't necessarily produce positive results. However, my willingness to move in that direction is the only way to obtain a new form of relatedness based on mutual respect and emotional maturity.

My conversations with divorced people who have dependent children make me extremely grateful that I do not have to contend with custody battles, visiting rights, and problems with child support checks. With a 50% divorce rate in today's society, learning to maintain emotional/spiritual equilibrium in the midst of constant disagreements over childcare is a problem facing the majority of parents in our country.

Without the help of God, the guidance of the Holy Spirit, and the compassionate love of Jesus Christ, I believe this is nearly impossible to accomplish. The suffering is immense and unavoidable for both parents and children, but does not have to cause total destruction to the human heart.

I now understand that allowing myself to feel overwhelming guilt and shame over the breakup of the marriage does not help and indeed hinders the process of healing. I believe it is important to say, "I'm sorry our choice causes pain for you," and admit that I am hurting too. I think it's necessary to allow each child to express his or her feelings regarding the divorce. Refusing to engage in open communications in an effort to avoid emotional outbursts can block continued growth in the relationship between parent and child. Trying to fill up the time with frantic activities instead of talking about what happened will not lessen the pain. Anyway, today's kids are too sophisticated to be conned by our efforts at pretense.

Sometimes divorced Christians try to bypass all these feelings in an effort to get to forgiveness. They may even cite scriptures in the attempt to encourage children to forgive the parents. The primary motivation behind this is often to relieve parental discomfort over the child's distress. If forgiveness is emphasized before the child is able to name and accept his feelings, much emotional damage can be incurred. A wise parent will encourage the child to express feelings without fear of ridicule, inhibition, or punishment. We can make it clear that, while the child may be punished for something he does, he will never be punished for what he feels. There are no bad feelings and the child is loveable no matter how he feels.

The words of Dr. Robert D. Wald, eminent child psychiatrist and faculty member of the University of San Francisco School of Medicine help to put this dilemma into perspective.

> We grow through adversity. We need not seek it out; whether divorced or not, we can all look back at moments when our lives were in utter chaos, desolation, and despair. Growth comes when we respond to adversity by stretching just an edge beyond our talent and experience. Growth is the result of the stretch. Happiness is the result of the striving.[7]

PRAYER

God,
you who are
Father and Mother to me,
I feel heartsick when I consider the pain
my choices are causing our children.
You know how much I love each of them.
To the best of my ability
I have tried to teach them
good values and Christian principles.
Our divorce
seems to be giving them
a different message.

I don't know how to explain all this
without becoming defensive.
At times I feel guilty and ashamed.

Please grant me wisdom
to know how to contend
with all the emotions
being generated
in me and in the children.
I ask your Holy Spirit
to guide me in being honest
about my feelings
so I may allow the children
to be honest too.
Remind me
that inner freedom
cannot develop when emotional denial
is being practiced.

Help me to teach them
to turn to you for comfort
so they may always
know your consolation in times of trouble.
I believe
each child came from you
and will return to you one day.
Therefore, I ask you
to fill in the empty places
where they may feel betrayed
or rejected by me or my former spouse.
Heal their broken hearts
and wounded spirits.
Give me the strength
to share the children.
Guard my tongue from remarks
critical of the other parent.

Jesus,
it was you who said,
"Let the little children alone,
and do not stop them from coming to me" (Mt 19:14).
To the best of my ability
I surrender my children into your care.
I believe you love them
even more than I do,
so I entrust them
to your tender love.

AMEN.

CHAPTER NINE

Finances

Confronting financial realities in the divorce process is often one of the most emotionally draining aspects of the situation. A sense of guilt may be felt when an attorney suggests economic strategies that seem harsh or demanding. Feelings of rage and anger may assail the one who believes he or she is being unfairly treated. Fear for the future welfare of oneself or one's children creates enormous tension. Long drawn out legal negotiations and confrontations are exhausting in this fight for financial security. Seldom are both parties satisfied with the final outcome. The financial settlements continue to affect couples long after the divorce agreement has been signed.

The word greed is often implied in divorce settlements. But the truth is few people really get rich on divorce, least of all women. A woman's income during the first year following a divorce drops, while her ex-husband's rises according to recent research. Lenore Weitzman concludes in her comprehensive study of divorce law:

> Women of all ages and at all socioeconomic levels experience a precipitous decline in standard of living within one year after divorce while their former husband's standard of living improves. Older women and women divorced from men in higher income tax brackets experience the most radical downward mobility.[8]

Therefore it becomes difficult to overcome the feelings associated with the allocation of money. Each time a threat to security is experienced it gives rise to all the angry, painful, panicky emotions once more. This may be accompanied by a desire for revenge or a wish to punish the former spouse. Of course, such fantasizing may cause a Christian who is trying to live a life of compassionate generosity to be overwhelmed with guilt and remorse for such thoughts.

Most therapists agree that financial security is a strong component for healthy emotional recovery following the trauma of divorce, but it is not a life raft readily available. "Divorce is a an accountant's game heavily weighted in favor of the monied spouse," stated one divorce attorney.

Finding the right attorney is not always an easy task. It can be equally difficult to accept the advice and counsel being given. One of the titles for the Holy Spirit is Advocate, a word meaning one who argues in my defense. I found it helpful to seek the wisdom of the Spirit for guidance and direction many times in the course of our divorce proceedings. Sometimes the needed counsel would come in the form of a magazine article or a TV program.

It is well to remember: feelings have no morality, they are neither right nor wrong, they just are. To experience strong feelings regarding perceived (and often legitimate) injustices is common to the human condition. Admitting to the anger, hurt, rage, etc., helps to facilitate dealing with it. Telling God and at least one other person about the strength of the feelings can lessen the pitfalls of stuffing, denying, and avoiding the issues. Relying on the Lord can bring renewed hope for the future by trusting in his graces.

PRAYER

Gentle Jesus,
you taught me
to trust in your providence
for all things.
You reminded me
that our Father cares
for the birds of the air
and the lilies of the field.
Nevertheless,
my heart is overwhelmed with fear
when I consider my financial needs
(and those of my children).
I admit to this lack of trust
in your ability to provide for me.
My faith is weak.
My courage fails me.
Grant me the strength to walk
through this emotionally draining experience.
Help me not to despair and lose heart.
Give me wisdom in confronting
the legal aspects of the divorce.

I believe
you can bring good
out of every situation,
but I need patience to endure
the often slowly grinding wheels of justice.
Thank you for holding me close to you
when my inner self feels so afraid.
Help me to rest in your care
for me and my loved ones.

AMEN.

CHAPTER TEN

Relatives

Divorce has a heavy impact on the entire family structure. Before the dust finally settles, nearly everyone from grandparents to the family dog gets into the picture. Sometimes the divorcing couple has to defend themselves more against interfering relatives than each other.

Often a family member is well intentioned and really trying to help. But frequently the announcement of a pending divorce signals barbaric behavior from ordinarily passive individuals. Anger and hostility can provoke nasty scenes where blame and accusations run rampant. Finger pointing and taking sides may create a kind of war zone atmosphere at family gatherings. The soon-to-be-divorced person needs to muster all the emotional support possible, and the closest relatives aren't always the best resource.

"My mother-in-law hardly ever spoke to me during my twelve years of marriage," said one woman. "But when Jack told her we were divorcing, she was on the phone every day, crying and pleading with me to reconsider. Jack and I were clear about the decision but we spent most of our time trying to comfort her." Divorce is definitely a family affair. A couple is choosing to do something that disrupts the whole structure. Even if the divorce was inevitable and desirable, someone in the family can react with a vengeance that puts Genghis Khan to shame.

The wife whose husband dies can expect lots of family support, personal attention, even financial aid. But the loss and grief attached to the divorce process doesn't usually inspire such compassion. It rocks the boat too much. It triggers feelings of failure, even in a culture that prides itself on granting personal freedom of choice. The state of California issues a pamphlet on divorce which states in part:

> Failure is not a popular word in America, yet every divorce statistic means two people have failed in life's most noble and important relationship — failed themselves, failed their children, failed their creator, and failed society. . . .

This is not a tract written by some fundamentalist sect, but by the Superior Court of a state government. It truly represents the deepest feeling of most Americans in spite of the seemingly more accepting attitude openly displayed. Divorce conveys failure resulting in a felt sense of shame which is at the bottom of most of the reflexive response to divorce. When a couple chooses to separate and divorce, other family members may also experience a sense of failure which triggers shame and promotes reactive behavior. The more *unconscious* the feelings, the more likely a relative will project the entire load onto the couple.

Recognition of the impact of divorce on the entire family structure helps to explain the uncivilized behavior, but it doesn't take away the feelings of abandonment and alienation experienced by divorced persons. "Mary's family always acted so friendly to me," shared one newly divorced man. "My sister-in-law always called me her favorite brother. But during the divorce proceedings she turned ugly and made up all kind of lies about our marriage." Unfortunately, such stories are all too common. The emotional strain of feuding family members added to a nervous system already on overload can make for many sleepless nights.

Learning to receive support from outside sources can be imperative to mental health. Again, turning to those who have been there and survived the trip can be of immense value. I still vividly recall having breakfast in Thousand Oaks, California with my friend Chuck, who had gone through a divorce several years earlier. Ben and I were in the beginning stages of separation and filing for divorce and I was a wreck. I sobbed through most of the meal while Chuck quietly let me feel my feelings. In the end he simply said, "You will make it through and be a better person for it. I don't regret my choice. It was the best thing we ever did for each other and I'd do it again if I had to." Hearing these words from one who knew the arena I was entering, gave me great courage in the weeks and months ahead.

When family members cannot or will not be supportive, there are many others who can fill in the vacuum. If the family of origin is emotionally unavailable, it's beneficial to create a family of choice made up of those who can provide strength and encouragement. Jesus Christ had a similar problem at the beginning of his public ministry when his relatives misunderstood what was happening to him.

He was still speaking to the crowds when his
mother and his brothers appeared; they were
standing outside and were anxious to have a word
with him. But . . . Jesus replied, "Who is my
mother? Who are my brothers?" And stretching
out his hand toward his disciples he said, "Here
are my mother and my brothers. Anyone who does
the will of my Father in heaven, he is my brother
and sister and mother" (Mt 12:46-50).

Jesus clearly demonstrated the bond being formed between himself and his followers. This family of choice had
become just as important as his family of origin (a concept
foreign to the Jews of that time who believed nothing
surpassed the strength of blood ties).

Jesus continued to stay connected to his blood relatives,
especially his mother. But he was often comforted by those
outside the family structure. It remains true today, no
matter how sophisticated society becomes, that divorce
will always be traumatic for everyone who touches our
lives. Parting from one with whom we formed strong
emotional and sexual ties spills over into the world around
us. No one can ever really do their own thing where
relationships are concerned. As the poet John Donne said,
"Everyone's death diminishes me because I am a part of
mankind."

PRAYER

Jesus,
you said those who did your will
were mother and brothers and sister to you.
My earthly family
does not completely understand
my decision to dissolve the marriage.

Help me to not
become overwhelmed when attacked
by the verbal accusations of loved ones.
Give me the insight
to understand their anger
and grief over my decision.
Comfort my broken-heartedness
over the feelings of abandonment
I am feeling.

Please send others into my life
who can be there for me
during this painful passage
just as you had many outside your family
who ministered to your needs.

Thank you
for the kind and supportive relatives
who have not taken sides.
Please bless them
as they have been blessing to us.

AMEN.

CHAPTER ELEVEN

Loneliness

Sometimes the loneliness of a divorcee is so oppressive it feels like it has a life of its own. It seeps into the corners and crevices of one's entire being with a sensation of overwhelming emptiness. We feel disconnected from everyone and everything — society, co-workers, relatives, friends — even from ourselves. Isolated and alone, we walk through the days and nights as if in a dream state where nothing seems real, and we pray to wake up at any moment.

"No one really understands the depth of my internal nothingness," I tell myself. Once my life seemed filled with meaningful relationships. My marriage appeared to offer a form of lifelong companionship. Rearing five children to adulthood provided ample opportunities for togetherness and shared experiences. More than two decades of active

Christian ministry garnered dozens of close relationships that have borne the test of time. Yet my newly acquired single status gave a sense of unreality to these connections. Was all my life merely an illusion?

The deepest emptiness occurred when I considered relating to God. The countless hours spent in communion with my creator, the father/mother God of my existence, now seemed hollow and unreachable. Even in the darkest moments of my life, I could always trust in the companionship and consolation of my eternal friend.

The psalmist cries out, "Where could I go to escape your spirit?" (Ps 139:7), but I sigh, "Where are you? Why do I no longer experience your consolation? Have I committed the unpardonable sin and ruptured the relationship between God and myself? Am I now damned for all eternity?"

Sometimes I even questioned whether God was ever there. Perhaps my spirituality was built on illusions and projections. The forms of prayer that always brought comfort now seemed to bring even deeper feelings of estrangement. My devotional practices appeared meaningless and repetitious. I hesitated sharing my hollowness lest others see this as a sign of God's disfavor. So I learned to pretend all was well on the outside, while experiencing unbelievable isolation from others, myself, and my God in my innermost being.

Loneliness is a form of distress more common than the common cold. Nearly everyone, divorced or not, experiences it in some form. Most divorced and separated people rate the feeling of loneliness as their greatest problem. One young woman, divorced at age 21, stated, "The fear of being alone and feeling that way for the rest of my life was overwhelming to me. It caused me to enter into some very destructive sexual behavior after my separation, just to fill in the emptiness."

The effects of loneliness have been somewhat ignored by behavioral scientists, thought to be merely a symptom of some other condition, such as depression. Only recently, impressed by evidence that loneliness is its own creature, have experts begun to study it. Dr. James Lynch, the director of the Psychosomatic Clinic at the School of Medicine of the University of Maryland has done impressive research documenting the medical consequences of loneliness. In his book, *The Broken Heart,* he writes, "In our fragmented society, the lack of human companionship and the sudden loss of loved ones is one of the leading causes of premature death, especially through heart disease."[9] His research underscores what every divorced person intuitively understands: the heart may be only a complex anatomical pump, but it is greatly influenced by human feelings and social situations.

Clearly, loneliness is not solitude, for we may be alone for long periods without feeling at all lonely. And we may feel suddenly, unaccountably lonely surrounded by loved ones without understanding why. Professor Robert Weiss, a sociologist at the University of Massachusetts at Boston, who has done more work on the subject than anyone in the country, says, "You are lonely when you feel there is nobody upon whom you can rely to augment you, especially in conditions of stress or threat." Also from psychologist Carin Rubenstein, who has designed tests to measure loneliness: "It is a feeling of missing something, of being without human attachments that you need."[10]

One divorced woman shared her insights, "It's when you feel, 'My God, there is *only me.*' I have never felt so lonely as when I was married. When things were black and he was drinking heavily and behaving like a dictator, I remember pervasively, constantly feeling: 'My God, it's terrible; and there is no one I can turn to, no one to help me; there is only me.' I know women are lonely after divorce, but I wasn't. I did all my leaving before I actually left."

People described the sensation of loneliness in a variety of ways: restless, miserable, bored, impatient, angry. The divorced and separated characterize it as a tension, an ever-present anxiety, helplessness, a sense of emptiness and distress, even panic, which even the kindest of friends can do little to cure.

Based on his research, Professor Weiss developed a theory of loneliness. Most of us need to feel at least two kinds of connection with the rest of the world. The first he calls emotional attachment — that central intimate tie that in our society is most commonly provided by marriage. The other need is for social integration — being part of a network, such as friends or community, whose members have common interests. Neither can compensate for the other, both are needed.

There is no magic cure-all for the affliction of loneliness. Desperately seeking others who can fill in the empty places is often disappointing when it fails to produce the desired results. The distinguished sociologist, David Reisman, has written:

> Loneliness is best cured by not going about it too strenuously, however great the loss which gave rise to it. In that sense it is like happiness, whose direct pursuit is self-defeating; for happiness, like emotional integration, is often the by-product of other activities. [11]

Loving relationships are important for our physical and emotional well being, but we cannot begin to cultivate them until we face the interior emptiness wrought by divorce. Seeking to prematurely fill up the hole will only give rise to further unhappiness.

Loneliness can have healing qualities when viewed as a time for introspection, reflection, and inner growth. Most of us complain that our lives are too busy. Time alone with ourselves and our God can reap great benefits. We seek to transform our desert of loneliness into a garden of solitude where rest and healing can be accomplished.

PRAYER

Eternal friend,
my sense of emptiness
threatens to swallow me up.
I am afraid of being alone,
of spending the remainder of my life
suspended in nothingness.
I feel separated
from all that formerly brought
connectedness and belonging.
This emptiness
threatens my relationship with you
for I no longer experience
the comfort of your presence.
In my rational thinking mind,
I believe you live in my heart
and will never leave me.
I recall moments
when all things seemed clear to me
and my heart sang
with the joy of union with you,
with others,
and with my self.
Now closeness
has all but disappeared.
Intimacy has given way
to isolation.

Jesus,
do not let my faith weaken

in these times
when everything seems so far away.
I meditate
on your experience with loneliness
in the garden of Gethsemane.
You were no stranger
to feelings of isolation
as you three times
begged your disciples to remain close to you
during your emotionally draining ordeal.
You graphically describe feelings
that mirror my own when you say,
"Wait here and keep awake with me" (Mt 26:38).
Your heart cried out for belonging
just as mine does.
Thus I believe you accompany me
through the lonely moments of my life
even when I fail to feel your closeness.
I rely not on my feelings of emptiness
to define our relationship.
I accept as truth
the words you speak to my heart,
"And know that I am with you always;
yes, to the end of time" (Mt 28:20).

AMEN.

CHAPTER TWELVE

Friendship

A recently divorced woman commented to me, "The most difficult part of my separation and divorce was not the loss of my spouse, but the loss of some long-term friendships. When people know you as a couple, it's very hard for them to relate to you as an individual."

She went on the describe how she felt rejected and avoided by some of her closest friends. "The ones I thought would be there turned their back on me and it really hurt. I was prepared to experience abandonment from my ex-spouse, but not from our friends. I ran into a woman in the grocery store who has known us for years and she couldn't seem to get away fast enough."

Such scenarios seem to be common after a divorce. Friends and acquaintances often take sides in deciding who was at fault. It usually isn't too hard to discern whose side they are on. Others find it difficult to know what to say regarding the break-up and so find ways to avoid conversation. This is similar to the behavior sometimes displayed toward a recently widowed person.

However, the most common reason for this seeming neglect on the part of former friends has to do with the newly acquired status as single. Traditional American society makes it very hard for the single person to fit into the structure. Parties, dances, and other social events ordinarily involve couples. (Although many churches are learning to provide singles' events, the majority of socializing revolves around the family structure.)

Also, a single person, but especially a divorced one, and most especially *a divorced woman*, presents a potential threat to other marriages. This subtle fear is the basis for much ostracizing on the part of friends and a source of much confusion to the newly divorced person.

Couples who are uncertain about their own marital relationship generally avoid getting too close to a divorcee. As one woman candidly remarked to me, "I thought you had a wonderful marriage and if divorce can happen to you it can happen to me too." I have come to accept the rejections of my former friends not as rejection of me, but as an unwillingness to accept me as a single person. I realize my divorce was a profoundly threatening event in the lives of some of my closest friends.

The Christian community, both Catholic and Protestant, can be particularly cruel to a fellow church member going through a divorce. This is especially true if the denomination employs strong teachings regarding biblical principles of marriage and separation. I have listened to extremely painful stories of rejection and severe mental abuse perpetrated by church officials and church members against those who chose to end a troubled marriage. Such measures, because they are initiated by fellow Christians, carry a heavy weight of judgment and shame for people who are already breaking under the strain of separation and divorce. The termination of community friendships can be devastating for one who is struggling to regain a sense of self-worth in the midst of divorce proceedings. I found the initial entry into singleness after thirty years of marriage was very frightening. I simply did not know how to relate. Very few of my friends were unmarried and most have grown children so the major portion of conversation revolves around family interests. The first time I visited with married friends, I was overwhelmed with emotional distress as I watched them interact with each other and their children. My heart ached as I recalled similar scenes in my own household. I longed to be back home with my ex-husband, surrounded by all our children. I managed to make it through the evening and returned home to cry myself to sleep. It was many months before I could accept another such invitation.

This experience led to the realization that I would have to supplement my old relationships with new friends who understood and accepted my singleness. It meant finding people with whom I could be fully honest with my thoughts, feelings, and emotions. I learned that a true friend doesn't seek mastery over another's life with reminders of what we should be. The real friend seeks a relationship that is mutually rewarding and enriching.

I've learned the importance of moving away from relationships that bring me down and increase feelings of shame about myself. Divorce recovery is enhanced when we surround ourselves with those who bring out the best in us and help us on the journey toward inner peace.

My life now consists of interacting with many well adjusted singles and married couples who model healthy social living and are teaching me to do the same. Learning to let go of the old patterns was the first step toward entering into a new adventure in relationships.

PRAYER

Jesus,
you seemed to value
friendships highly
during your time on this earth.
You invited twelve
to be your apostles.
Many others accompanied you
on the journey from town to town.
Three men,
Peter, James, and John
were always close
at important moments
during your public ministry.
Yet, in your time of need,
only one of these friends
remained at your side.

Lord,
I too feel deserted and rejected
by those who were my friends.
I miss the sense of togetherness
that characterized these friendships.
I feel abandoned
at a time when I most need to know
the love and support of others.
Sometimes, my attempts
at reconnecting with old friends
brings more heartache than consolation.
My life has undergone so many changes
and friends do not always understand
the direction I am taking.

Help me to let go
of the relationships
that are no longer
life-giving for me
or for my former friends.
Grant me wisdom
to discover new forms of relating
and develop new support systems
compatible with my singleness.
Thank you for remaining close
during this time of transition
as I accept the truth of your words,
"I shall not call you servants any more;
. . . I call you friends" (Jn 15:15).

AMEN.

CHAPTER THIRTEEN

Intimacy

Everyone is born with a huge capacity to love and be loved, to give affection and receive affection, to touch and to be touched. Marriage is one of the socially acceptable channels for answering these basic human needs. Two people publicly commit themselves to live in a love relationship with one another during their earthly journey.

However, within the human heart there lurks an equally strong inclination to avoid closeness. Each of us retains a fear that the union which seems so compelling, warm, and tender, so beautiful, can also be a trap to retard personal freedom and growth. We struggle between these two forces, striving desperately to enjoy fully the fruits of love, yet fearing it will engulf and negate our personality.

One could define intimacy as a state of knowing that results from walking through fear. To be intimate with another means facing the fear of engulfment and risking the possibility of being wounded by the beloved. Vulnerability is always a gamble.

Ideally, when two individuals publicly state their intention to maintain a marriage relationship, they are proclaiming their willingness to walk through fear in order to connect emotionally, physically, and spiritually. Each person is vowing to maintain relatedness no matter what happens in this life.

When a marriage terminates in divorce, the shattering of illusions regarding intimacy often leaves a sense of disillusionment about relatedness. The trauma of divorce commonly fosters feelings of rejection, abandonment, and betrayal. The myth of happily ever after is seen as some cruel joke played on the unsuspecting parties. The hopes and dreams for togetherness that marked the wedding day now lie unrealized and unreachable.

Dissolution of a marriage greatly affects the trust level of each spouse. There may even be a conscious or unconscious vow never again to get that close to another. It takes time for trust to regenerate. Many find it difficult to believe that trust will ever again be possible. Some become callous and cynical, declaring love to be a farce and marriage a trap. Such protestations are generally born from the fear of being wounded. Others refuse to allow themselves to develop any types of friendships, choosing to erect high emotional barriers around themselves. We can't force ourselves to become more trusting in relations with others. It evolves from within the secret recesses of the heart as we permit the Lord to heal the areas of hurt.

From a Christian standpoint, intimacy is an essential component for life. The God who created the universe knows each creature intimately, "Before I formed you in the womb, I knew you" (Jer 1:5). My identity as a child of

God comes from knowing who I am because God validates my personhood. "I know you through and through from watching your bones take shape while you were formed in secret, knitted together in your mother's womb" (see Ps 139).

The Bible says, "I have called you by your name, you are mine" (Is 43:1). To know a person's name in the Hebrew culture was to know the personality, character, and destiny of another. Therefore, the creator's knowledge, acceptance, and love of me are part of a whole. Jesus illustrates this truth with the metaphor of the vine and branches. The fruit of love is spiritually produced because there is oneness and connectedness.

The Christian view of oneself comes from within, not outside the personality. Failures in intimacy result from misunderstanding this fact. Society promotes the illusion that my half person needs your half person in order to become whole. Each attempts to draw a picture of the self by looking into the eyes of the loved one. A once popular song, "You're Nobody 'til Somebody Loves You," clearly demonstrates the confusion surrounding relationships. With no real sense of self emerging from an inner core of connectedness with God, unhealthy enmeshment evolves. The partners believe survival is impossible without the other. Such a union is doomed to fail since it places far too many demands for identity on the shoulders of the loved one.

Divorce can lead to greater awareness of the role of God in establishing one's identity *if* we take the opportunity to get to know ourselves. One who does not have an honest relationship with the self finds it impossible to have a healthy connectedness to another. It is therefore important to set aside time to foster awareness of our inner being. Time spent in quiet reflection brings into focus the message that a broken relationship does not mean the loss of self. Asking God to reveal our real nature can begin to heal brokenness by providing a new source of grace for self-respect.

At some point in time, we need to make a conscious effort to reconnect with the world around us and cease allowing fear to dominate our relations with others. We can gently begin to open up to possibilities for relationships like a tiny flower opens one petal at a time to the sunlight. As Gandhi once said, "If you trust, you will be hurt, but if you don't trust, you will never learn to love."

PRAYER

Dearest friend,
many of my attempts
at relatedness to others
have proven fruitless.
I am now frightened of getting close
because the risk of further rejection,
abandonment, and betrayal seems overwhelming.
I contemplate the words of scripture,
"You must love your neighbor as you love yourself."
It makes me aware
that the first step toward true intimacy
must be in learning to love and accept myself.
Please open my mind and heart
to hear your affirmation of my nature.
Give me the grace to draw close to you
so I may become more conscious of your love.
Help me to believe you desire intimacy with me
so I can walk through the fear
of becoming close to you, to myself, and to others.

AMEN.

CHAPTER FOURTEEN

Dating

The break-up of a marriage, especially between two people who believed their union was forever, produces great barriers to new relationships. The fear of getting involved again and the sense of failure often give rise to isolation and escapism.

Yet, in spite of these overwhelming feelings, three out of four divorcees eventually remarry again. The human desire for intimacy is very strong. To gain closeness, there must be willingness to overcome the reluctance to risk further hurt. Each person meets this challenge in a different way by letting go of defenses and becoming vulnerable once more.

Initially following a divorce, the resulting chaos and confusion often produces what some counselors describe as "crazy time," a time when a formerly balanced individual engages in a variety of "wild" behaviors calculated to restore lost self-esteem. A man may experience a number of one-night stands to prove his masculinity is still intact. A woman may enter into an affair in an effort to feel desirable. The result of this acting out is generally further chaos and confusion.

The feelings associated with the sense of abandonment, loss, and rejection must be faced, owned, and accepted as part and parcel of divorce recovery. Conscious awareness of these emotions and impulses makes unhealthy behavior less likely.

Ordinarily it doesn't take long before a person realizes that promiscuity will not answer the cry for intimacy. Conversely, the one who chooses instead to isolate and avoid relationships also may come to the same conclusion. God created us to love and this love comprises more than physical expression.

Disengaging from the fears of intimacy can be very precarious. There are no guarantees that future friendships won't end up in disaster. Despite the best intentions, the complexities of becoming vulnerable are extremely intricate.

The dating scene introduces a variety of problems for the newly divorced person. The prospect of going out with another after many years of marriage can be very unnerving. "The idea of dating produced panic attacks in me," shared one woman divorced after fifteen years of marriage. "What would we talk about? What would be expected on the first date? Society today is much different from my former dating days, and I'm really scared of the single life."

It's important to note that men and women think of love and intimacy differently. For many men, sex leads to love and intimacy, while women usually see sex as an outcome of love and intimacy. One way to prevent misunderstanding concerning the role of sexuality is open discussion regarding the Christian view of sex outside of marriage. Open discussion with eligible dating partners clears the air by informing the other person exactly what our values are.

Finding suitable people to date can also be quite a challenge. Christian singles groups may be helpful, and many churches provide opportunities for meeting others in this way. Getting involved in volunteer work is another way to discover people with similar interests. Many couples have met, dated, and married through participating in volunteer activities. For the children of divorced parents, the prospect of Mom and Dad socializing with the opposite sex can sometimes be more disruptive than the divorce itself. Children feel threatened by the potential relationship developing between the parent and an outsider. They already feel abandoned by the break-up of the marriage and this insecurity can cause violent reactions against any new parental friendships. Adult children also find it hard to accept that their folks would want or need the attention of the opposite sex at their *advanced* age. It can be a real balancing act to continually reassure your children of your love while at the same time asserting your new found independence. Again, open communication in listening to a child's protests can be beneficial. Often a stand for freedom must be taken. As one person shared, "I told my children I could only continue to be a loving parent if I also felt loved, and my friendship with the other person was producing this fruit."

PRAYER

Creator of my heart,
Jesus taught the world
that you are a God of love.
He said
we were to love one another
just as he loved us.
However,
my attempts at loving relationships
have often been disastrous.
My sense of failure in marriage
makes me frightened of trying
to get close again.
I fear being rejected.
I cannot bear more heartache.
Please grant me the courage
to walk through these fears.
Heal my memories
of previous relationships
that I may dare to risk intimacy once again.
Guide me to choose friendships
that will be mutually healthy and life-giving.
Keep me far from associations
that would further wound my inner being.
Give me wisdom
to know the places and situations
that might provide
the right relationships for me.
Help me to be patient
when I feel clumsy
and inept with the process
of developing socializing skills.

Above all,
help me to regard my singleness
as a blessing, not a curse.
May I not seek companionship
as an escape from loneliness
but as a means of becoming
more loving toward you,
toward others,
and toward myself.

A M E N .

CHAPTER FIFTEEN

Self-Esteem

Divorce has a profound effect on a person's concept of self. The sense of identity has undergone a tremendous shock. The first time I filled out a credit card application, I became completely unnerved over the question about marital status: married/ single/ divorced/ widowed? I wanted to lie and check off *widowed* just so I wouldn't have to admit being a *divorcee*. A feeling of being unwanted and unattractive were uppermost in my mind.

In my conversations with other divorcees, several divorced men shared their feelings of uprootedness after leaving the family home and no longer living with the wife and children. Each felt confused about his identity. As one man articulated it, "I'm a displaced husband and an absent father...so who am I?" Resolving the question of self-worth and self-esteem is an essential component in divorce recovery.

In 1988 the state of California commissioned a twenty-nine-member panel of mental health professionals to study the effects of poor self-image in the social structure of today's society. After three years of intense deliberation they issued an exhaustive report. Their work clearly details the necessity for developing governmental programs to increase healthy self-esteem. A National Council on Self-Esteem was formed as a result of this study and other states are following California's lead by adopting some of the successful elements of the research data.

One of the most startling concepts to emerge from the report is that self-esteem can serve as a social vaccine. Once introduced into the system (like a bacterial vaccine into the body) it can help ward off the lure of crime, violence, substance abuse, teen pregnancy, child abuse, chronic welfare dependency, and educational failure.

The task force chose to define self-esteem as, "Appreciating my own worth and importance, and having the character to be accountable for myself and to act responsibly toward others." This sense of innate worth is really the God-given right of every human person. It is the inner conviction that believes, "I am treasured, valuable, cherished, respected, and worthy of being loved." It is an inherent truth which no one has a right to destroy.

Pia Mellody, in her book *Facing Codependence*, describes self-esteem as "the internal experience of one's own preciousness."[12] It is a positive personal attitude toward life and the people around me.

Virginia Satir, the family therapist who pioneered the psychological aspects of healthy self-image taught that feelings of worth could only flourish in an atmosphere where individual differences were appreciated, mistakes were tolerated, communication was open, and rules were flexible. This type of environment exists in a nurturing family and gives life to those who are fortunate to receive it.

The humiliation encountered in a broken marriage takes a high toll on one's inner resources. The devastation regarding belief in one's own goodness is enormous. The emotional destruction is often so great that recovery can only be accomplished by seeking counseling from one who understands the depth of the pain.

Most of the divorced people I interviewed experienced a severe blow to their self-esteem resulting from the marital break-up. Even those who believed divorce was the only answer to a sick marriage still felt ashamed and guilt-ridden by the decision. Often these feelings of self-hatred can lead to unhealthy addictive behavior in an effort to dull the pain.

In a previous chapter, I discussed the problems encountered in parenting following a divorce. The difficulties are compounded when the divorced parent's self-esteem is badly damaged and she takes it out on the children. Child abuse is directly related to a parent's feelings of self-worth. When a person does not feel good about herself, the tendency is to be more punitive and to display less patience. Restoring a sense of self-worth is absolutely essential to maintaining healthy relationships. Believing we are valued and empowered, we convey a sense of confidence at home as well as in the workplace, causing us to treat others with the same respect.

The road to achieving this sense of value requires an honest willingness to admit our feelings about ourselves. A support group of others who are recovering from broken relationships can be a very helpful tool. One of the axioms of Twelve Step programs states, "Recovery is something one has to do *oneself*, but one does not have to do it *alone*." There must be a safe environment where feelings can be ventilated without fear of criticism. Openly admitting any self-loathing begins the process of letting go of any erroneous self-images — the new wine cannot be put into the old wineskins.

Self-awareness is painful. The first time I went to a Twelve Step meeting for Adult Children of Alcoholics, I was amazed at the openness displayed by some of the members as they described personal feelings of shame, hatred, and anger toward themselves. I was certain they were exaggerating the high degree of negativity until I began searching my own heart and found much of the same material.

Healing begins to occur when we take the time to really examine the way we view ourselves. It requires commitment to personal growth and continued self-care. It doesn't happen spontaneously, nor is it linear. Ordinarily, the path is a continuing journey of highs and lows, with the highs becoming lower and the lows getting higher. It may not always be easy, but it is rarely uninteresting.

I often hear remarks about the pain involved in getting well after divorce, but my experience has shown it to be a lot easier to become emotionally healthy than to live in a marriage with no hope for life.

PRAYER

Spirit of truth,
please help me
obtain an accurate picture
of the image I carry of myself.
In many ways
I honestly do not like
the person I see inside of me.
I blame myself
for the break-up
of my marriage.

If only I were more loving,
more caring,
more generous,
then all would be well.
This self-hatred
colors everything around me
with a dark veil of mistrust.
How can I love others
when I have so little love for myself?

Give me the courage
to confront my inner distortions
by sharing my confusion
with those who can affirm my goodness.
As I learn to admit
my lack of self-esteem,
grant me the grace
to know my own preciousness.
Help me to treasure my existence
as a pearl of great price.

AMEN.

CHAPTER SIXTEEN

Forgiveness

The well-known phrase, "to err is human, to forgive divine," strikes a blow to the heart of every divorced person. The impact of emotions generated by separation and divorce gives ample excuse for continued bitterness and anger against the former spouse. The pain associated with legal battles over finances, child support, and custody of dependent children makes the very thought of forgiveness absurd. Getting even is the name of the game and thinking up ways to make the other party miserable can occupy many waking hours.

Being angry over unjust and unfair treatment by a former spouse, by family members, by the lawyers connected with the case, and by the court system is a normal and healthy response to the pain. Not being able to control much of what is happening is a great drain on the emotions. Anger is a necessary and appropriate response to the feelings of powerlessness generated by divorce.

For healthy divorce recovery to take place, it is very important to allow oneself to feel all the feelings associated with this devastating loss. Many Christians try to skip over all the uncomfortable feelings by jumping into forgiveness too soon. Thus they ignore, avoid, or postpone much of what needs to be embraced and integrated into their spiritual lives.

In the other extreme, it is possible to never let go of the desire to get even. Such a person almost delights in wallowing in self-pity and endless recounting of the list of offenses. Healing the wounds of the past is nearly impossible if there is an unwillingness to begin the forgiveness process.

At some point the divorced person must make a conscious decision to stop hating and begin living once more. Forgiveness is a decision, not a feeling. You don't necessarily feel kind, generous, or loving toward the former spouse. Such tender emotions may never surface again. But it is possible to decide to cease clutching the pain and let it go.

You cannot always control what happens to you, but you can control reaction to the happenings. You can refuse to allow victimization by another person to break your spirit, make you physically ill, or perhaps even shorten your life. Most medical professionals know that anger, worry, and stress can make you sicker than a virus. The Chinese have a way of saying it, "You cannot stop the birds of worry from flying over your head, but you can stop them from building a nest in your hair." Hatred is like an acid. It can do more harm to the container in which it is stored than to the object on which it is poured.

Positive action to overcome negativity can be taken and forgiveness is usually the first step. Sometimes the damage done by the broken relationship and its subsequent fallout is so great that a divorced person cannot fully agree to forgive. In such situations I suggest taking a half step rather than a full step. Simply pray, "Lord, help me to be willing to be willing to forgive." Such a prayer opens the door ever so slightly, yet gives God permission to begin to soften the heart and heal the pain.

Often one needs to forgive not only the former spouse, but also the relatives and friends who caused emotional suffering. The mechanism is the same; the process can only start with the invitation, "Lord, I want to forgive_____."

Perhaps it may be helpful to write a letter to the former spouse (or to others who may have offended us) stating that forgiveness is in process. Such a letter may never be posted in the mail, but the catharsis of the writing can bring much needed relief.

It can be especially difficult to forgive when there is consistent interaction with the former spouse concerning finances, children, distribution of property, etc. Each encounter tends to open the old wounds once more. In such situations we can ask the Lord's protection for our sensitive emotions and for grace to forgive each time we find it necessary to meet.

Often the person most difficult to forgive in the process of divorce recovery is oneself, especially if we initiated the divorce proceedings or if we believe the marriage could have survived had we tried harder. "If only I had loved her more." "I know it was mostly my fault." "God must surely judge me as a lousy Christian." "I hate myself because of the divorce."

Such bashing of oneself only brings further misery to one already filled with pain. Mental health cannot be achieved until we say, "I made some mistakes, but it is not the end of the world. I forgive myself for not being perfect." It takes practice to stop the inner voices of self-criticism. It's also not unusual for a spiritual person to feel some anger toward God regarding the outcome of the marriage relationship. Perhaps we prayed, fasted, and asked others to intercede for a healing of the union. We may feel betrayed by God because our prayers and good works seemingly were to no avail. Confronting and acknowledging such feelings of disappointment in God can open the door to allowing the light of the Spirit to grant new perspectives on the situation.

During his agony on the cross, Jesus demonstrated the importance of forgiveness when he cried, "Father, forgive them; they do not know what they are doing" (Lk 23:34). He had the power to retaliate by calling on the angels to avenge him, yet he chose the path of forgiveness. When we are overcome with bitterness and anger toward others, ourself, or God, we can ask the Lord to grant the gift of forgiveness to our hearts. In some mysterious way, this prayer is always answered for those who are sincere.

All who seek to walk the way of peace must learn the way of forgiveness. The divorced person has ample opportunity to practice this virtue.

PRAYER

God of love,
illumine my inner being
with the light of the Spirit
and reveal any lack of forgiveness
that may be lurking in the shadows.
Help me to be willing to forgive
no matter how deeply I was wounded
by the rejection, slander, cruelties,
or betrayal surrounding my divorce.
Please increase my awareness
of any root of bitterness
toward my former spouse.
To the best of my ability
I desire to forgive _____ from my heart.
Please give me the grace
to be willing to stop holding onto
the old hurt feelings and resentments.

May I extend
the same consideration
toward myself
and cease any self-hatred
that threatens my mental health.
I forgive myself
for not being perfect
and for any lack of love
demonstrated toward my former spouse.
Also, I desire to forgive you,
my creator,
for my perceptions
concerning seemingly unanswered prayer
with regard to the outcome of the marriage.

I know that "the heavens are as high above earth
as [your] ways are above [my] ways,
[your] thoughts above [my] thoughts" (Is 55:9).
I want to trust again in your wisdom
to direct my life and to watch over me,
and I want to see more clearly
the purpose behind these events of my life.

Please give me the grace
to continue the practice of forgiveness
so you can always bless me
with your forgiving love.
Thus the promise made to me by Jesus
will be fulfilled,
"if you forgive others their failings,
your heavenly Father
will forgive you yours" (Mt 6:14).

AMEN.

CHAPTER SEVENTEEN

Surrender

Surrender means acute awareness and acceptance of reality, the acceptance that this is the way it truly is! We cannot really move into the future until we let go of the past.

To surrender means not to be protective of others.
It's to let our loved ones face their own reality, the consequences of their own decisions.
To surrender means to stop trying
to control others.
It's to use my energy to become what I dream
I can be.
To surrender is not to regret the past.
It's to grow and live for the future.
To surrender is to stop denying.

It's to become more accepting of reality.
To surrender does not mean to stop caring.
It means I can't do it for someone else.
To surrender is to fear less and give up guilt
and feelings of inadequacy.
It's to love and accept both myself and others more.[13]

The pathway toward recovery from a broken marriage is marked with countless twists and turns along the road. Often we seem to take three steps forward and four steps back with strong emotions threatening to jeopardize the trip. At each juncture on the trail we can choose to let go of the past and move on with life or stay stuck with feelings of hopelessness, regret, and sorrow. We can trust that God will be there for us on every step of the journey or we can avoid seeking divine intervention and try to go it alone.

To choose life is exceedingly frightening because we seldom know what that choice may entail. A trapeze artist can monotonously swing back and forth on the bar high above the circus ring. However, to move on he must first let go of his safe comfortable bar and momentarily hang in mid-air, trusting someone will be there to catch him. The sensation of helplessness as he tumbles through the air is a normal part of the process toward reconnecting.

Letting go begins to happen when we acknowledge powerlessness regarding many aspects of our separation and divorce. It means seeking outside help when feelings become overpowering and reality appears distorted. Letting go may entail detaching from unhealthy groups or relationships that impede the healing process. It usually involves finding support groups and life-giving friendships for companionship on the way.

Letting go means trusting in God's unconditional and never failing love in the midst of confusion and doubt. The entire Bible is a testimony to God's faithfulness to his promises toward those who trust in him. No matter how the Israelites strayed from his loving care, Yahweh was constantly reaching out to them through his prophets. "We may be unfaithful, but he is always faithful, for he cannot disown his own self" (2 Tm 2:13). Faith is built on experience. Trust levels increase as we let go of fear and begin to notice a new sense of peace.

Part of my letting go involved detaching from my ministry at Our Lady of Divine Providence House of Prayer in Clearwater, Florida, and accepting an invitation to relocate in California from my friend Juanita Meller, who was then the administrator for the Southern California Renewal Communities. To do so meant facing the unbearable pain of separating from my two daughters, my son-in-law, and my grandson who live in Florida. It entailed leaving numberless friends and neighbors. It involved detaching from my home and most of my belongings. I was terrified!

My friend Linda agreed to join me in driving across the country from Florida to California. The week before we were to leave found me in New Jersey teaching a workshop on healing prayer. My heart was heavy with grief as I prayed over each participant at the end of the sessions. Outwardly I was trying to appear normal, while inside I was dying. I was nearly finished with the prayer time when I found myself looking into the face of a radiantly smiling black woman. She said her name was Beatrice and she handed me a card with a note of prayer requests. Several hours later on the flight back to Tampa, I read the verse written on the card. It was from a bookmark found in the prayer book of St. Teresa of Avila.

> Let nothing trouble thee,
> let nothing frighten thee,
> all things pass away,
> God never changes.

Patience obtains all things,
nothing is wanting to him who possesses God.
God alone suffices.

To this day I believe Beatrice was an angel sent from God to give me this message. I was still feeling terrified but it gave me renewed courage to continue on the pathway.

My daughter Beth was another earth-angel during the painful days of packing my treasures and loading the car. I sobbed almost constantly and she stayed with me through it all, even though her own heart was breaking. On the day I left, she took me to lunch and gave me a pep talk similar to the one I had given her when she went away to college in Miami. Her parting gift was a card and note placed under the floormat of my car. The card said:

You're Never Alone

You've had a rough time of it, and no one can know how hard it's been for you, but now it's time to move on, to look to tomorrow again instead of yesterday. So, as you make a start on your new life, remember that you can count on my friendship for support. . . . And as long as you're in need of help or a shoulder to lean on and a reassuring word. . . as long as I'm here . . . you're never alone.

I still carry this in my Bible as a constant reminder of Beth's love and affirmation. The words of Beth's card and St. Teresa's bookmark didn't relieve all the fear, grief, and doubt in my heart, but gave me the courage to keep moving on in spite of the inner conflicts. Painful feelings remained in my heart for many months and still rise up when I least expect to encounter them. Surrender implies a continuing acceptance of the reality of our situation while believing in hope for better things in the future. Such faith is a daily exercise of trust. "Life demands from you only the strength you possess. Only one feat is possible, not to have run away," wrote Dag Hammarskold.

The well-known Serenity Prayer, written by the theologian Rienhold Niebuhr, is one of the most powerful surrender prayers ever written.

PRAYER

God, grant me
the serenity
to accept the things I cannot change;
the courage
to change the things I can;
and the wisdom to know the difference.
Living one day at a time,
accepting hardship as a pathway to peace,
taking, as Jesus did,
this sinful world as it is,
not as I would have it.
Trusting that you
will make all things right
if I surrender to your will,
so that I may be
reasonably happy in this life
and supremely happy with you
forever in the next.

AMEN.

EPILOGUE

If some fairy godmother offered to remove all our deepest sorrow and pain, but would also remove all memories of the years gone past, would we accept the offer?

An ancient Greek legend gives a clue to the choice we would probably make. It tells of a woman who came down to the River Styx where Charon, the gentle ferryman, stood ready to take her to the region of the departed spirits. Charon reminded her that it was her privilege to drink of the waters of Lethe, and if she did she would forget all that she was leaving behind.

Eagerly she said, "Will I forget how I have suffered?" To which Charon responded, "But remember you will also forget how you have rejoiced." Then the woman said, "Will I forget my failures?" The old ferryman replied, "And also your victories." Again the woman said, "Will I forget how I have been hurt?" "You will also forget," countered Charon, "how you have been loved."

The woman paused to think the matter over, and the story concludes by telling us that she did not drink the waters of Lethe, preferring to hold on to the memory even of her suffering and her sorrow rather than surrender the remembrance of life's joys and loves.

The Christian can best understand this story by reflecting on the resurrected body of Jesus Christ. He emerged from the tomb after three days and appeared to his followers with the marks of crucifixion still visible in his hands, feet, and side. The suffering Jesus experienced on the earth was not removed when he entered his risen body. The pain was transformed yet still recognizable.

Likewise, the woundedness we've experience in this life is never completely removed. Our gentle God touches the sorrows so they no longer overwhelm us, yet we still remember what happened. Somehow an inner change takes place allowing us to perceive each situation in a new light.

An old Yiddish proverb consoles us with the reminder, "Not to have had pain is not to have been human." The pain passes, the memories remain; loved ones leave us, but the experience of love endures. We are richer for having paid the high price of being connected, vulnerable, and intimate with God, with others, and with ourselves.

APPENDIX

Annulment

To the best of my ability I have tried to write this book as a spiritual guide for all Christians who suffer the heartache of separation and divorce. While non-Catholic readers may find it difficult to understand some of this appendix, I chose to include it because I view this procedure as an important tool for divorce recovery for those of us who embrace Roman Catholicism. Perhaps it will clarify questions for Christians who do not belong to the faith community of the Catholic church or provide some new insights for those baptized Catholics who do not understand or accept the church's theology and canonical legislation regarding marriage.

There is a common misconception that the Roman

Catholic church penalizes divorce by excommunicating (denying the sacraments) to a divorced person. There is no church penalty for divorce. As long as you do not remarry without annulment, you may receive the sacraments and participate in the full life of the church. The words of Pope John Paul II's apostolic exhortation on the family (Dec. 15, 1981) express compassion and concern regarding the confusion surrounding this misconception:

> . . . I earnestly call upon pastors and the whole community of the faithful to help the divorced and with solicitous care to make sure that they do not consider themselves as separated from the church, for as baptized persons they can and indeed must share in her life. They should be encouraged to listen to the word of God, to attend the sacrifice of the mass, to contribute to works of charity, and to community efforts in favor of justice, to bring up their children in the Christian faith, to cultivate the spirit and practice of penance and thus implore, day by day, God's grace. Let the church pray for them, encourage them, and show herself a merciful mother and thus sustain them in faith and hope.

The Catholic church believes that marriage, celebrated by two baptized persons, is a sacrament. A sacramental marriage is a permanent, faithful union meant to reflect the unity of Jesus Christ and his love for all people. The *Pastoral Constitution on the Church in the Modern World* defines marriage as

> an intimate partnership established by the creator and qualified by his laws. It is rooted in the conjugal covenant of irrevocable personal consent. . . . Through this union the partners experience the meaning of oneness and attain to it with growing perfection day by day (*Gaudium et Spes*, 48).

According to the church's view of marriage, if one or both of the spouses is unable to meet the requirements for this community of *conjugal life*, a sacrament has not been constituted. If at the time when marital consent was given, either spouse lacked sufficient use of reason, suffered from some grave lack of discretion or judgment concerning matrimonial responsibilities that are to be mutually given and accepted, or was not capable of assuming the essential obligations of matrimony due to psychological reasons, the union is not considered a sacramental marriage. A stable, permanent, faithful bond has not been established and there is no sacramental union without a community of love and life.

However, the church cannot allow marriage after divorce until the previous, presumably valid, sacramental bond is sufficiently examined and a decision made about the nullity of that sacramental bond. Annulment is the process in the Roman Catholic church that allows divorced Catholics to have their marriage "set aside" by the church. It is not the Catholic church's form of divorce as some mistakenly view the process. Divorce is the result of civil court proceedings whereby married persons become legally separated and the marriage is declared over. In declaring the nullity of a marriage, the church is stating that it was not a sacramental bond from the very beginning. When the church declares the *nullity* of a marriage, it is stating that a particular element required for valid matrimonial consent was lacking at the time of the wedding, and so the marriage was not valid.

A declaration on nullity extends renewed privileges to Catholics. If they have remarried this means they can receive the eucharist again. If they desire to remarry the sacrament of matrimony can be celebrated.

Whether a Catholic is "in or out" of the church after divorce or remarriage often affects many aspects of that individual's life, such as attendance by the children at a parochial or public school, religious education of the children, inclusion of the church in an individual's will or trust, planned place of burial, choice of a hospital, charitable contributions to Catholic institutions, attendance at Mass, and participation in the sacraments.[14]

In spite of the importance of annulment in putting to rest these questions, fewer than ten percent of divorced Catholic couples petition the church to set aside their previous marriage even though nearly eighty percent will enter into a second marriage. Many prefer to join the ranks of "fallen away Catholics" rather than face the sometimes rigorous demands of the annulment procedure.

The church makes no judgment on the legality of the civil divorce but is concerned only with nullifying the sacramental bond between those married in the Catholic church. Not being a canon lawyer, I won't attempt to explain all the legal or moral aspects of the process of nullity. There are several excellent and easily readable books cited at the end of this book which assisted me in the preparation of my own case.

I was initially petrified by the thought of going through the annulment process. The very word struck terror in my heart. I had heard stories from persons who had been denied their petition by the tribunal set up in each diocese to hear such cases. I didn't want to be criticized by those who erroneously believe divorced individuals purchased annulments from the church much like the granting of indulgences in the Middle Ages. Also, it appeared to be a lengthy and complicated ordeal and the thought of adding another burden to my already overloaded emotional state seemed absurd.

Yet close friends and advisors, including my wise and gentle spiritual director, urged me to look into the process.

After several months of dragging my feet, I made an appointment to discuss the situation with my pastor. The monsignor is a delightful man with an abundance of Irish wit and wisdom. He scheduled our meeting for 6 *a.m.* in the rectory, stating, "By that time half the day is gone so let's not waste a minute of the Lord's precious time."

His friendly manner immediately quieted the pounding of my heart as he deftly explained the process to me in simple and understandable terms. After listening to my perspective on the reasons for the failure of my marriage, he agreed to help me with the required paperwork. He said I would have to do a lot of reflecting and honest evaluating of my marital history, but I must always remember, "the tribunal is not sitting in judgment of you or your self-worth, only the ability of you and your former spouse to enter into a validly holy and committed covenant relationship." He summed it all up with these words, "I can make you no promises concerning the outcome of your petition, but I can promise you a fair hearing by the archdiocesan tribunal based on the information you and your witnesses provide."

Ben believed the civil divorce was sufficient and, therefore, was not interested in pursuing a ruling from the church in this matter. However, he agreed to cooperate with the process knowing it had much meaning for me.

Eighteen months after submitting the necessary paperwork, the annulment was granted. My initial reaction was one of overwhelming gratitude to God and to all who were instrumental in bringing this to pass. Subsequently I experienced a wave of great sadness, much stronger than the pain I felt when the civil divorce was handed down. Realization hit deep within my being, it was really *over* and the church agreed with the choice we had made in dissolving the union.

I wept long and loud. Sometime later my friend Josie found me where I had been sitting since reading the tribunal letter. She had gone through a similar situation following her divorce and annulment, so she knew how to be a companion through the pain. When the waves of sorrow abated, a sense of freedom began to permeate my heart. Something was lifted and deep peace prevailed.

From a spiritual perspective, the annulment process provided me with a profound framework for healing the pain of divorce. When Jesus gave St. Peter the keys to the kingdom of heaven, he stated, "Whatever you bind on earth shall be considered bound in heaven; whatever you loose on earth shall be considered loosed in heaven" (Mt 16:19). When the church declared my marriage to be "set aside" it somehow loosed me from my former spouse and broke any spiritual bond holding us together in unhealthy ways.

It is very difficult to undertake the required procedures. It is disturbing to reveal some of the intimate details of the marriage relationship. It is bothersome to dredge up remembrances. Yet the end result brings a resolution for much of the inner conflict and helps to heal some of the woundedness caused by the marital break-up.

The discipline of answering the questionnaire about the history of my marriage helped to clarify confused thinking regarding the relationship between Ben and me. I began to recognize an overview of our life together that made the reasons for divorce more obvious. My basic personality type usually avoids pain by stuffing it deep inside and distracting myself with outer activity. The annulment procedure forced me to ponder some sensitive issues and gave me a resource for uncovering many hidden feelings. By seeing the marriage as seriously flawed from the beginning (the church's definition of an invalid marriage) my emotional reaction began to have more focus. The simple statement at the end of the process sums it up better than I ever could: there were conditions that prevented the couple from making a binding commitment.

The church of Jesus Christ is always called to be the great healer, the source of God's mercy and reconciliation. Therefore, her ministry to the separated and divorced is nothing less than the fulfillment of her role of compassion toward the needs of wounded people.

PRAYER

Lord,
I come to you
with many doubts and fears
concerning my connectedness
to you and to the church.
I sometimes do not understand
the rules and regulations
that govern
the religious practices of my faith.
Please help me
to obtain correct information.
Let me not be confused
by my own or others' misconceptions
regarding the laws of the church
or erroneous Bible interpretation.
Please heal my heart
from any wounds of rejection
received from priests, nuns, deacons or others
who represent church authority to me.

Grant me the ability
to forgive those who
knowingly or unknowingly
treated me with harshness.
Give me guidance
in approaching the annulment process
and help me discern

if this is the best path
for me to take.
If I make this choice,
grant me the courage
to face the truth
about myself and my marital history
knowing the truth will always lead me closer to you.
Lord, I believe healing is possible
and all things, even divorce,
can work unto good.

A M E N .

NOTES

1 Henri Nouwen, *Out of Solitude*, Notre Dame: Ave Maria Press, 1974.

2 Fran Ferder, *Words Made Flesh*, Notre Dame: Ave Maria Press, 1986, p. 97.

3 Harriet Goldhor Lerner, *The Dance of Anger*, New York: Harper & Row, 1985, p. 189.

4 John Bradshaw, *Healing the Shame That Binds You*, Deerfield Beach, FL: Health Communications, 1989.

5 Merle A. Fossum and Marilyn J. Mason, *Facing Shame: Families in Recovery*, New York: W. W. Norton, 1989.

6 Diane Fassel, *Growing Up Divorced*, New York: Pocket Books, 1991.

7 Quoted in Mel Krantzler, *Creative Divorce*, New York: Signet Books, 1973.

8 Lenore Weitzman, *The Divorce Revolution*, New York: The Free Press, 1985.

9 James Lynch, *The Broken Heart*, New York: Basic Books, 1977.

10 Carin Rubenstein, "Loneliness, More Common Than the Common Cold," Redbook: Nov. 1980.

11 David Reisman, quoted in "Loneliness, More Common Than the Common Cold," Redbook: Nov. 1980.

12 Pia Mellody, *Facing Codependence*, San Francisco: Harper & Row, 1989.

13 Sharon Wegscheidre-Cruse, *Choicemaking*, Pompano Beach, FL: Health Communications, 1985.

14 Joseph Zwack, *Annulment: Your Chance to Remarry Within the Catholic Church*, San Francisco: Harper & Row, 1983.

FURTHER READING

Relationships

Fisher, Bruce. *Rebuilding: When Your Relationship Ends*. San Luis Obispo, CA: Impact Publishers, 1987.

Galipeau, Steven A. *Transforming Body and Soul: Therapeutic Wisdom in the Gospel Healing Stories*. Mahwah, NJ: Paulist Press, 1990.

Mellody, Pia. *Facing Codependence*. San Francisco: Harper & Row, 1989.

Rock, Leo P. *Making Friends With Yourself: Christian Growth and Self-Acceptance*. Mahwah, NJ: Paulist Press, 1990.

Schaef, Anne Wilson. *Escape From Intimacy*. San Francisco: Harper and Row, 1989.

Spaniol, LeRoy, and Lannan, Paul. *Getting Unstuck: A Workbook for Moving On After Divorce*. Mahwah, NJ: Paulist Press, 1984.

Wegscheider-Cruse, Sharon. *Learning to Love Yourself: Finding Your Self-Worth*. Pompano Beach, FL: Health Communications, 1987.

Wegscheider-Cruse, Sharon. *Choicemaking*. Pompano Beach, FL: Health Communications, 1985.

Woititz, Janet. *Struggle for Intimacy*. Pompano Beach, FL: Health Communications, 1985.

Divorce Recovery

Cosgrove, Melba, and Bloomfield, Harold. *How to Survive the Loss of a Love*. New York: Bantam Books, 1976.

Krantzler, Mel. *Creative Divorce*. New York: Signet Books, 1975.

Trafford, Abigail. *Crazy Time: Surviving Divorce*. New York: Bantam Books, 1988.

Grief

James, John W., and Cherry, Frank. *The Grief Recovery Handbook.* New York: Harper and Row, 1988.

Ripple, Paula. *Growing Strong at Broken Places.* Notre Dame, IN: Ave Maria Press, 1986.

Ripple, Paula. *The Pain and the Possibility.* Notre Dame, IN: Ave Maria Press, 1988.

Rupp, Joyce. *Praying Our Goodbyes.* Notre Dame, IN: Ave Maria Press, 1988.

Shame

Bradshaw, John. *Healing the Shame That Binds You.* Deerfield Beach, FL: Health Communications, 1989.

Kaufman, Gerhen. *Shame: The Power of Caring.* Rochester, VT: Schenkman Books, 1980.

Middelton-Moz, Jane. *Shame and Guilt: Masters of Disguise.* Deerfield Beach, FL: Health Communications, 1990.

Loneliness

Lynch, James J. *The Broken Heart: Medical Consequences of Loneliness.* New York: Basic Books, 1977.

Morrison, Douglas A. and Witt, Christopher P. *From Loneliness to Love.* Mahwah, NJ: Paulist Press, 1989.

Anger

Ferder, Fran. *Words Made Flesh.* Notre Dame, IN: Ave Maria Press, 1986.

Lerner, Harriet Goldhor. *The Dance of Anger.* New York: Harper & Row, 1985.

Children

Fassel, Diane. *Growing Up Divorced: A Road to Healing for Adult Children of Divorce.* New York: Pocket Books, 1991.

Annulment

Brunsman, Barry. *New Hope for Divorced Catholics.* San Francisco: Harper and Row, 1989.

Zwack, Joseph P. *Annulment: Your Chance to Remarry Within the Catholic Church.* San Francisco: Harper and Row, 1983.

Self-Esteem

Toward a State of Esteem, (the 160-page report by the California Task Force) can be ordered from: Bureau of Publications, California State Dept of Education, Box 271, Sacramento, CA 95802-0271.

Video Tape Series

The Truth Will Set You Free. A spiritual recovery program of teachings by Barbara Shlemon and Fr. Jack McGinnis, designed to aid recovery from life's losses and issues of guilt and shame. This six part video series also has a companion workbook to assist the individual or groups with recovery guides. For further information contact: Recovery Publications, 1201 Knoxville St., San Diego, CA 92110-3718 (1-800-873-8384).